Brilliant guides

What you need to know and how to do it

When you're working on your computer and come up against a problem that you're unsure how to solve, or want to accomplish something in an application that you aren't sure how to do, where do you look? Manuals and traditional training guides are usually too big and unwieldy and are intended to be used as end-to-end training resources, making it hard to get to the info you need right away without having to wade through pages of background information that you just don't need at that moment – and helplines are rarely that helpful!

Brilliant guides have been developed to allow you to find the info you need easily and without fuss and guide you through the task using a highly visual, step-by-step approach – providing exactly what you need to know when you need it!

Brilliant guides provide the quick easy-to-access information that you need, using a table of contents and troubleshooting guide to help you find exactly what you need to know, and then presenting each task in a visual manner. Numbered steps guide you through each task or problem, using numerous screenshots to illustrate each step. Added features include 'See also...' boxes that point you to related tasks and information in the book, while 'Did you know?...' sections alert you to relevant expert tips, tricks and advice to further expand your skills and knowledge.

In addition to covering all major office PC applications, and related computing subjects, the *Brilliant* series also contains titles that will help you in every aspect of your working life, such as writing the perfect CV, answering the toughest interview questions and moving on in your career.

Brilliant guides are the light at the end of the tunnel when you are faced with any minor or major task.

Author's acknowledgements

Pearson and I go way back. I'm starting to feel like part of a family. If I'm not mistaken, this is our 13th or 14th book together in fewer than five years, and I am very proud of the relationships we have fostered during that time. It's been an amazing run, with lots of opportunities and successes for us all.

I would like to thank Steve Temblett, Katy Robinson and Helen Savill for guiding me through this book. They are all thoughtful, kind, and great leaders, and let me do just about anything I want to do and in almost any time frame. I couldn't ask for any better publishing team.

As my faithful readers know, I have a family to thank too. I have my Dad, Cosmo, Jennifer and Andrew, and a few others who are related in various ways through them. My mom passed away in February of 2009, and while expected, it hit me harder than I thought it would. Everyone recovers from such tragedies, though, and generally we end up stronger for it in the end. I can say that's true for me, as I have grown intellectually and spiritually, and am faster to forgive and slower to anger. Mom would be proud. I wish she were here to see how I've grown and how well I'm taking care of Dad (who turned 90 in 2010).

I am also thankful for Neil Salkind Ph.D. of the Salkind Literary Agency. He is my agent, but he is also my friend and mentor. He and his team read my contracts and manage my minor disputes and complaints, they watch my royalty statements and payments, and Neil secures books deals and does all of the other things you'd expect from an agent, but he's much more than that: he's a friend. We'll be celebrating ten years together in 2011, during which we've published 40 or so books together. That's a long time in agent–writer years.

Finally, thanks to you, my most awesome readers and fans. May you find this book helpful and easy to understand, and I sincerely hope it assists you in getting the very most out of your laptop or netbook. My door is an open one . Feel free to contact me anytime at *joli_ballew@hotmail.com*, and be assured I'll write you back. I love to hear from my readers.

Publisher's acknowledgements

We are grateful to the following for permission to reproduce copyright material:

Screenshots

Page 77 from Google, © 2011 Google – Map data, © 2011, Google, Tele Atlas; page 115 from Yahoo!, Reproduced with permission of Yahoo! Inc. © 2011 Yahoo! Inc. Yahoo! and the Yahoo! logos are registered trademarks of Yahoo! Inc.; page 123 from CNN.com, courtesy CNN; page 199 from Skype™; page 294 from Flickr, reproduced with permission of Yahoo! Inc. © 2011 Yahoo! Inc. Yahoo! and the Yahoo! logos are registered trademarks of Yahoo! Inc.

In some instances we have been unable to trace the owners of copyright material, and we would appreciate any information that would enable us to do so.

About the author

Joli Ballew (Dallas, Texas) is a technical author, a technology trainer and website manager. She holds several certifications, including MCSE, MCTS and MCDST. Joli is also a Microsoft MVP (four years running), and attends the Microsoft Summit as well as the Consumer Electronics Show in Las Vegas, Nevada (US) every year to stay on top of the latest technology and trends. In addition to writing, she teaches computer classes at the local junior college, and works as a network administrator and web designer for North Texas Graphics. Joli has written more than a dozen books for Pearson's In Simple Steps and Brilliant series and is currently writing even more titles. In her free time, she enjoys yard work, exercising at the local gym, and teaching her cats, Pico and Lucy, tricks.

Dedication

Mom, been almost two years. We all miss you deeply.

Contents

Introduction

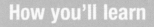

Welcome to *Brilliant Laptops*, a visual quick reference that will help you get the most you can from your laptop or netbook. In this book you'll learn how to use your mobile device effectively, including how to access the Internet, lengthen battery life, play and manage media, store and manage data, and use online resources to keep your data safe and secure. As you can see from the Contents, there's much more than this, too. This book assumes you have a new netbook or laptop, so here I'll discuss Windows 7 as the installed operating system. If you have an older device, you can still use this book effectively, you may just find the exact steps and features differ slightly (or aren't available).

Find what you need to know – when you need it

You don't have to read this book in any particular order. We've designed the book so that you can jump in, get the information you need, and jump out. To find the information that you need just look up the task in the table of contents or Troubleshooting guide, and turn to the page listed. Read the task introduction, follow the step-by-step instructions along with the illustration, and you're done.

How this book works

Each task is presented with step-by-step instructions in one column and screen illustrations in the other. This arrangement lets you focus on a single task without having to turn the pages too often.

How you'll learn

Find what you need to know – when you need it

How this book works

Step-by-step-instructions

Troubleshooting guide

Spelling

Step-by-step instructions

This book provides concise step-by-step instructions that show you how to accomplish a task. Each set of instructions includes illustrations that directly correspond to the easy-to-read steps. Eye-catching text features provide additional helpful information in bite-sized chunks to help you work more efficiently or to teach you more in-depth information. The 'For your information' features provide tips and techniques to help you work smarter, while the 'See also' cross-references lead you to other parts of the book containing related information about the task. Essential information is highlighted in 'Important' boxes that will ensure you don't miss any vital suggestions and advice.

Troubleshooting guide

This book offers quick and easy ways to diagnose and solve common problems that you might encounter, using the Troubleshooting guide. The problems are grouped into categories that are presented alphabetically.

Spelling

We have used UK spelling conventions throughout this book. You may therefore notice some inconsistencies between the text and the software on your computer, which is likely to have been developed in the US. We have, however, adopted US spelling for the words 'disk' and 'program', as these are commonly accepted throughout the world.

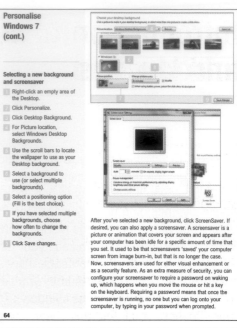

Troubleshooting guide

Introduction to netbooks and laptops

Introduction

If you have just purchased a new laptop or netbook, congratulations! If you're still on the fence, perhaps reading this chapter will help you decide what's best for you. If you've had your laptop or netbook for a while and are experiencing slow response times, software problems, or feel you're bogged down with programs you don't need or that you're lacking software you do need, we can help you there, too. Whatever your situation, you'll find this chapter helpful and a great place to start.

First, let's lay out the facts. Laptop computers are smaller versions of their desktop counterparts. They often do everything a desktop computer will, and offer portability. Netbooks, in contrast, are smaller versions of their laptop counterparts. They won't do everything a laptop will, and often don't offer as many features. Throughout this book we may use laptop or netbook or both to describe a portable computer. Unless specifically noted, the topic at hand refers to both.

In this chapter you'll learn a little about your (new) netbook or laptop. First, you'll discover what the major differences are between them. Then, you'll discover a little about Windows 7, the operating system most probably installed on your new computer. Finally, you'll learn about third-party programs you'll want to get, and how to clean up your new computer by uninstalling third-party programs you don't want (but which were installed by the manufacturer).

What you'll do

Show the Welcome Center

Explore the Getting Started window

Explore jump lists

Explore libraries

Access Devices and Printers

Explore Windows 7 programs

Download and install Windows Live Essentials

Get Microsoft Security Essentials

Uninstall an unwanted program

Distinguish between laptops and netbooks

▶

! **Important**

If you haven't purchased a netbook or a laptop yet and aren't sure what to get, visit a computer store and spend some time typing on one. If you have large hands, you may want to opt for a larger laptop.

Laptops and netbooks are both types of portable computers. They differ in many ways, though. The easiest way to distinguish between a laptop and a netbook is to look at its size and weight. Laptops are larger and weigh more; netbooks are smaller and weigh less. Because laptops are larger, they have the extra physical space required to offer a CD/DVD drive; because netbooks are smaller, they do not and don't generally come with one. Larger laptops also have more room for additional RAM (random access memory), may have larger hard drive capacities, offer larger screens, and offer larger keyboards and track pads. Netbooks, which are smaller, obviously have smaller components (screen, track pad, keyboard and hard drive).

Both laptops and netbooks have the major components you'll need and expect in a computer, including but not limited to Ethernet ports, Wi-Fi hardware, USB ports, and a place to plug in external speakers and headphones. Both keyboards offer the usual array of keys, including Function and Page Up and Page Down keys. Both come with netbook-specific hardware, including a power button on the keyboard and a bay to hold the battery.

Most new laptops and netbooks come with Windows 7 preinstalled. Windows 7 is an operating system, and all computers have one. If you purchased an older laptop or netbook, it may have Windows XP or Windows Vista on it, though. This book covers Windows 7, but you can still learn quite a bit even if your computer runs something else.

There are various editions of Windows 7 and each has distinct features. Windows 7 Basic has fewer features than Windows 7 Home Premium, and Home Premium has fewer features than Professional or Ultimate. Most laptops will come with Windows 7 Home Premium, fewer with Professional, and even fewer with Ultimate. Most netbooks will come with either Home Basic or Home Premium, depending on their price and on-board resources such as RAM and other system components. To find out what operating system you have, click Start, right-click Computer and click Properties.

!

Important

If you find you have Home Basic, you may be able to upgrade to Home Premium. Click Get more features with a new edition of Windows 7 to find out whether your computer is compatible.

```
Computer
              Open
              Manage
Control Pan

              Map network drive...
Devices and   Disconnect network drive...

              Show on Desktop
Default Prog  Rename

Help and Su
              Properties
```

View basic information about your computer

Windows edition

Windows 7 Home Premium

Copyright © 2009 Microsoft Corporation. All rights reserved.

Get more features with a new edition of Windows 7

If you find your netbook has Windows 7 Home Basic, you won't have all of the Windows 7 features available to many Windows 7 users. For instance, while you can join a homegroup in Home Basic, you can't create one, and Home Basic does not have Windows Media Center while Home Premium and higher editions do. That's OK, though – you don't need or want all of that in a lower-end netbook anyway, because the computer may not have the required system resources.

i

For your information

The editions of Windows 7 build on each other. Basic has the fewest features, Home Premium has more, and Professional and Ultimate have even more than that.

Additional components ▶

In addition to the operating system, your laptop or netbook probably came with third-party programs preinstalled. These may be trials of software for you to try out, or they may be fully fledged programs unique to the manufacturer. On rare occasions a manufacturer will install anti-virus software and include a subscription for a year, but for the most part what you'll get is 'trialware'. Because of this, most software that's installed on top of the operating system is stuff you're not going to want to keep. These programs take up hard disk space and can run in the background using system resources, sometimes without your knowledge.

In addition to items you don't want, some programs you simply don't need. Windows 7 comes with a music program (Windows Media Player) and depending on your edition, Windows DVD Maker, Media Center, and more. There's no sense in duplicating what you already have with something else the manufacturer has included. On a small netbook, system resources are very valuable and should not be squandered on programs you don't use or need. Later, you should decide whether you want to keep these additional programs or not, and uninstall them if you decide you don't want them.

Unfortunately, laptops and netbooks running Windows 7 are missing a few major software components. Windows 7 does not come with an email program, for instance, nor does it come (by default) with any anti-virus software. You'll also find you probably need an image-editing program, instant messaging program, or perhaps even a video-calling program (such as Skype). Most of the time, you can add this software for free, though, so it's really only a matter of knowing what you want, finding it and installing it. We'll show you where to get this software at the end of this chapter.

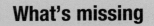

What's missing

1

Overcoming laptop and netbook limitations

▶

Finally, it's important to understand and work to overcome the limitations of laptops and netbooks. These aren't desktop computers, and getting the most from yours requires a bit more effort on your part than working with a desktop PC does.

One major problem is that mobile computers can be easily lost, stolen or damaged. To overcome this limitation, always make sure you keep good backups, protect your computer with a strong password, and secure it when possible in a car boot, locked to a desk or on your person. More safeguards are outlined in Chapter 15 on safety and security. You can also store important data on internet servers, so that if your computer is stolen your data won't be.

Another limitation is a lack of physical resources. Expensive laptops don't have this limitation, but lower-end laptops and almost all netbooks do. You may not have enough RAM to run multiple programs efficiently. You may not have enough hard drive space to store all of the data you're used to storing. You may not have a CD/DVD drive for installing programs or watching movies. You'll have to work around these limitations as they arise. Throughout this book you'll learn how to deal with these limitations.

We're assuming that your computer has some version of Windows 7 on it. You will use Windows 7 to find things you have stored on your computer, connect to the Internet, send and receive email, and surf the Web, among other things. You don't need to be a computer guru or have years of experience to use Windows 7. Its interface is intuitive. The Start button offers a place to access just about everything you'll need, from photos to music to email; the Recycle Bin holds stuff you've deleted; and the Desktop Gadget Gallery offers gadgets you'll almost certainly want to access, such as a clock, the weather and news headlines. But there's a lot more to it than that! The best way to get to know your new netbook or laptop is to explore the operating system.

Important

!

Windows 7 comes in several editions and computer manufacturers often add their own touches. As a result, your screen may not look exactly like the ones you'll see in the screenshots in this book (but it'll be close).

Explore the Getting Started window

The first time you started Windows 7, the Getting Started window may have opened. Here you can learn quite a bit about Windows 7 in very short order. There are options to find out what's new, personalise Windows, add new users and more. Often computer manufacturers add their own listings and links to help you learn about your computer and the applications they've installed on it, as well as links to their own Help files or website.

You can learn many things from the Getting Started options, but the items you'll be most interested in now are:

- Go online to find out what's new in Windows 7 – access information regarding what's been added since Windows Vista, including, but not limited to, using the Action Center to keep your computer secure and maintained, taking advantage of new navigation features, using the new Windows HomeGroup to set up your home network, using Device Stage to see device status, using Internet Explorer 8, and accessing new features such as Windows Touch.

- Personalize Windows – change the picture that appears on your Desktop, change your screen saver, personalise sounds and apply system-wide themes.

- Transfer files and settings from another computer – learn about and use Windows Easy Transfer, an application included with Windows 7 that helps you transfer user accounts, files and folders, program settings, Internet settings and Favorites, and email settings, contacts and messages from an older computer to your new one.

- Back up your files – open Windows Backup and back up important files once or on a schedule.

- Add new users to your computer – learn how to secure your computer with user accounts for each person who will access it. If two people share one PC, each can have his or her own user account, where documents, email, photos and other data are secure and completely separate. You can also customise settings and set up parental controls here. If you have a network, you can add users to allow access to the data on your computer from another computer securely.

Important

What you see in your Welcome Center may differ from what you see here.

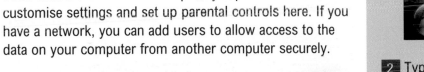

Showing the Welcome Center

1 To open the Getting Started window, click the Start button.

2 Type Getting Started.

3 Click Getting Started.

Explore the Getting Started window (cont.)

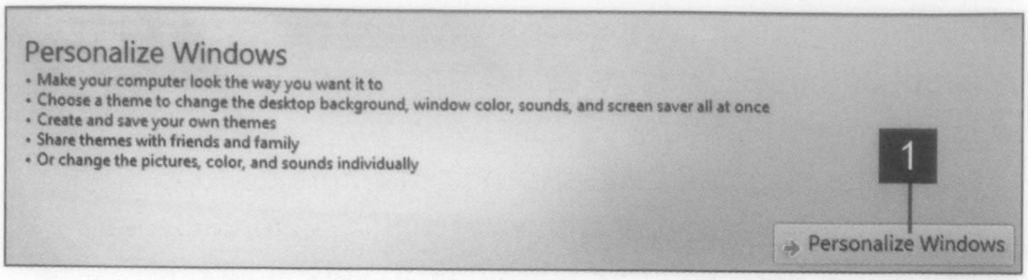

Exploring the Getting Started window

1 With the Getting Started window open, click Personalize Windows.

2 Notice the top pane changes to reflect your choice.

3 Later, you could click Personalize Windows to modify your copy of Windows 7, although you'll learn how to do that in Chapter 4.

Personalize Windows
- Make your computer look the way you want it to
- Choose a theme to change the desktop background, window color, sounds, and screen saver all at once
- Create and save your own themes
- Share themes with friends and family
- Or change the pictures, color, and sounds individually

1

→ Personalize Windows

?

Did you know?

To close any window, click the X in the top right corner.

While the Welcome Center can help introduce you to Windows 7, help you personalise it and even show you how to transfer data from one computer to another, there are a few features that are so special they deserve their own callout here. These are features that will really excite you, especially if you're just moving up to Windows 7 from Windows XP.

◀ **Utilise new Windows 7 features**

1

Windows Search

Every place you look in Windows 7, there seems to be a Search box. Click the Start button and there's a Search box. Open any Explorer window, the same. Open any personal or public folder, ditto. You can use these search boxes to find anything on your computer quickly, including personal data, media, programs, and Windows 7 utilities and features. There's even a Search box in the Windows Help and Support window!

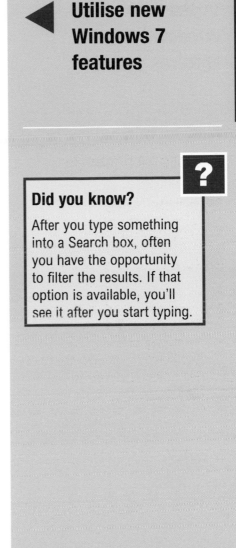

Did you know?

After you type something into a Search box, often you have the opportunity to filter the results. If that option is available, you'll see it after you start typing.

Jump lists

The Taskbar (the transparent bar that runs across the bottom of the screen) offers icons for programs that are open, as well as programs you've opted to pin there permanently. This isn't anything incredibly new. But what is new are the jump lists that are now available from those icons. A single right-click offers access to recently played songs, recently viewed pictures and recently edited documents, as well as common tasks you'd probably want quick access to.

See also

Learn about pinning items to the Taskbar or the Start menu in Chapter 4.

Utilise new Windows 7 features (cont.)

Exploring jump lists

1 Right-click any icon on the Taskbar.

2 Review the options.

3 Click any option to jump to it.

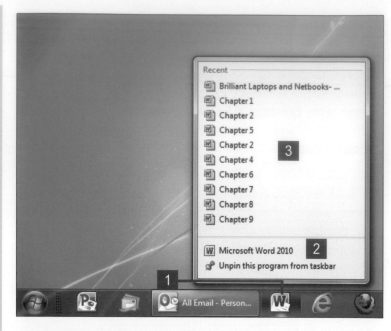

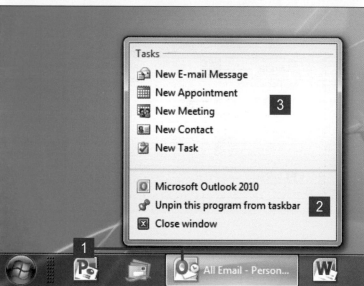

Libraries

Libraries are new, too, and offer easy access to similar data stored in multiple places on your hard drive (or even on your network). The Documents library offers quick access to documents stored in your personal Documents folder as well as documents in the Public Documents folder. The same is true for the Pictures library, Music library and Videos library.

You can also create your own library, or add folders to any library, including the default libraries. This enables you to have easy access to like data, even if it is not the same type of data. For instance, you could create a library called My Home Business and in it include access to invoices and documents (stored in the Documents folder), pictures and videos (stored in the Pictures and Videos folders) and specialised folders you've created such as Clients, Artwork and Tax Information, as well as various other folders and subfolders.

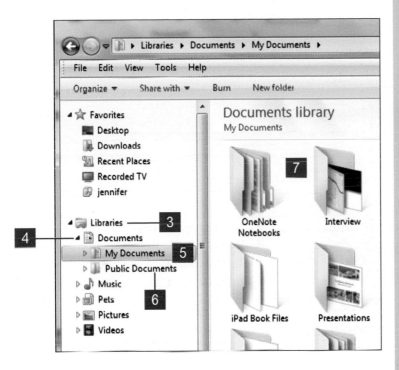

Exploring libraries

1 Click Start.

2 Click your user name.

3 Move the mouse to the Libraries section in the left pane.

4 When the arrows appear, click the arrow beside Documents.

5 Click My Documents.

6 Click Public Documents.

7 Explore what is in those libraries.

Utilise new Windows 7 features (cont.)

Homegroups

When you have more than one Windows 7 computer on a network, you can create a homegroup for them. Homegroups make sharing data easier by configuring all of the sharing options automatically. The homegroup is also protected by an automatically generated password and is allowed only on private networks for extra security.

Change homegroup settings

This computer belongs to a homegroup.

Share libraries and printers

☑ Pictures   ☑ Music   ☑ Videos

☐ Documents   ☑ Printers

How do I share additional libraries?   How do I exclude files and folders?

Share media with devices

☑ Stream my pictures, music, and videos to all devices on my home network
    Choose media streaming options...
    Note: Shared media is not secure. Anyone connected to your network can receive your shared media.

Other homegroup actions

    View or print the homegroup password
    Change the password...
    Leave the homegroup...
    Change advanced sharing settings...
    Start the HomeGroup troubleshooter

Save changes   Cancel

Shake, Snap, Peek

Shake, Snap and Peek are three of the most exciting new features of Windows 7. Try all three now:

■ Shake – to utilise Shake, open several windows and position them in various places on your computer screen. Click the title bar of one of them and, while holding down the left mouse key, shake that window from left to right. All of the other open windows will fall to the Taskbar and be minimised. Shake again to restore them.

■ Snap – drag any window from its title bar to the left or right side of the screen. It will snap into place, taking up exactly half of the screen automatically. Position one window on the right side and one to the left to easily drag and drop files between two windows.

- Peek – open several windows and then position the mouse at the bottom right corner of the screen. This will allow you to 'peek' at the desktop behind all of the open windows. This is especially useful if you have gadgets on your Desktop. Peek is shown here.

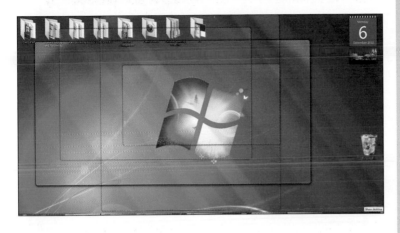

Action Center

The Action Center keeps an eye on your computer and informs you when there are problems. It also looks for solutions to problems you've previously encountered, even if you ignored those problems at the time. When solutions are found, you'll be informed. You'll want the Action Center to be healthy and to show no problems. If you see problems, you'll want to resolve them quickly.

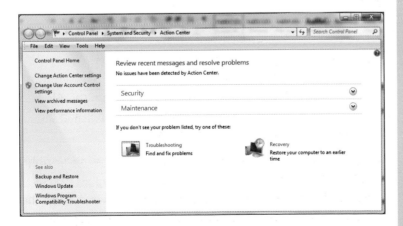

Utilise new Windows 7 features (cont.)

Accessing Devices and Printers

1 Click Start.

2 Click Devices and Printers.

3 Review the devices. Right-click any connected device.

4 Click Properties.

Devices and Printers

Devices and Printers shows all connected devices and often previously connected devices as well. If the device is connected, you can view its status, see its Properties page and more. You can troubleshoot device problems here, too.

Network and Sharing Center

The Network and Sharing Center offers information about your network and a place to troubleshoot network problems. Here's a healthy network and the options you'll see in the Network and Sharing Center. You can do a lot of things from the Network and Sharing Center, including configuring sharing settings, enabling media streaming, setting up a new network, viewing all network devices and more.

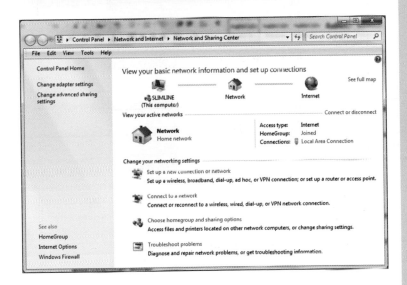

Explore Windows 7 programs

Windows 7 comes with some programs that you'll find quite helpful. There are the usual suspects you're probably familiar with, including Games, Paint, WordPad and Media Player. But you'll also find the Desktop Gadget Gallery, Media Center, Windows DVD Maker and more. The best way to see what's installed on your computer is to explore the Start menu's All Programs list.

Exploring Windows 7 programs

1 Click Start.

2 Click All Programs.

3 Look for the following programs and open them if you wish:

   a. Desktop Gadget Gallery.

   b. Windows Anytime Upgrade.

   c. Windows DVD Maker.

   d. Windows Media Center.

   e. Windows Media Player.

   f. Windows Update.

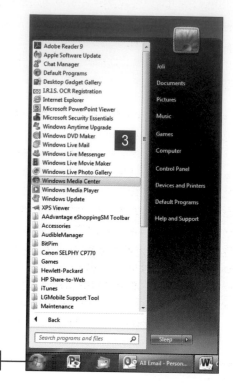

Did you know?

It's easy to see whether you can upgrade the Windows 7 operating system to another edition – just run the Windows Anytime Upgrade tool.

Important

If you have Home Basic you won't have all of these programs.

You know that your Windows 7 laptop or netbook does not have everything you need to work effectively. There's no email program, no photo-editing program, no anti-virus software, no office application and no video-editing software. But how do you know what you really need, and how can you possibly decide among the myriad offerings? There's a lot to consider when it comes to filling in the gaps. First and foremost, you have to work within the limitations of your computer. If you have a big, fancy, expensive laptop, you can pretty much install and do what you want. However, if you have a less robust laptop or a netbook, you have to be much more careful and put a little more thought into it.

Consider this: sure, there's no video-editing software installed on your computer, but does your little netbook even have the resources required to edit video? Probably not – you'd need 4 GB of RAM to edit video effectively. So you've answered the question 'What video-editing software should I get?' quickly and easily: none. You can also get by without other software – for instance, you could check your email at a website and forgo installing an email program entirely. You could use online tools such as Google Docs instead of purchasing and installing an expensive and resource-intensive application such as Microsoft Office. And when you do opt for software, you can install web-based and compatible applications – Microsoft's Live Essentials suite of applications, for instance. They're free, enhanced for Windows 7 and don't use too many computer resources.

We're going to look at some of these options in depth throughout this book. For now, though, let's make a list of programs you may want to acquire and programs we feel you *must* acquire, and learn a little about cleaning up some of the mess already on your laptop or netbook, even if it's new.

Know the programs you need to obtain

Downloading and installing Windows Live Essentials

1 Visit www.explore.live.com.

2 Click Windows Live Essentials.

3 Click Download Now.

4 During the installation process, select only the components you know you'll use.

5 When prompted, get a Windows Live ID if you don't have one.

There are some programs that you really should have, even if you have limited resources available:

■ Email management – although you can check your email from an online web space such as *www.live.com* or *www.aol.com*, we contend it's best to install a program so that you can manage your email at your computer. We suggest Windows Live Mail.

■ Photo editing – although you can edit photos on your desktop computer and transfer them to your portable one, we suggest you install a simple photo-editing program so that you can easily upload, edit, organise, manage and access images on your portable computer. We suggest Windows Live Photo Gallery, part of the Windows Live Essentials suite.

■ PDF reader – you'll need to read PDF (Portable Document Format) files. You can get the free Adobe Reader for this.

■ Instant messaging – if you use an instant messaging program already, go ahead and install that messaging program on your new laptop or netbook. If you don't want it to run all the time in the background, configure it so that it does not start with Windows.

Options	
Personal	**Sign in**
Sign in	General
Contacts	☐ Start Messenger when I log on to my computer
Messages	☐ Open the main window when Messenger signs in

■ Anti-virus/anti-spyware – even though anti-virus and anti-malware software will use system resources and will probably noticeably slow down your computer, you have to have it. We've had good luck with Microsoft Security Essentials and have not noticed a resource problem, even on our bare-bones netbook.

Getting Microsoft Security Essentials

1 Visit *www.microsoft.com/ security_essentials/*.

2 Click Download Now.

3 Follow the instructions to download the program.

4 Verify your computer is protected and up to date after installation.

■ Office applications – if you plan to work at your laptop or netbook, you'll have to install an office program. We suggest you try the online options, such as Google Docs and Microsoft Office Live Workspace. If these don't suit your needs, try the smallest edition of Microsoft Office that will work for you or try OpenOffice.org.

Know the programs you need to obtain (cont.)

These programs we consider to be must-haves:

- Windows Live Essentials – this free suite of applications runs efficiently on laptops and netbooks, and offers a simple way to manage email, send instant messages, blog, edit photos and more. The programs work together, too.

- Windows Live Office Workspace – this free workspace offers the ability to create documents online, store sensitive data on secure online servers and collaborate with people (whom you choose) all over the world.

- Microsoft Security Essentials – this free anti-virus, anti-adware, anti-malware software runs quietly in the background, is not intrusive through pop-ups or warnings, updates itself automatically and protects your computer from Internet threats.

- Skype – if you try and don't like Windows Live Messenger for video calling, or you have friends who use Skype, we suggest this for keeping in touch. Since almost all laptops and netbooks come with a video camera, it's certainly a must-have.

- Various programs as the need arises – if you find you need to play a QuickTime movie but find you don't have the software, by all means install QuickTime. Just configure it so that it does not start when Windows does but rather runs only if you start it manually. You may also need other programs, including the free PowerPoint Viewer from Microsoft, iTunes, mobile phone synching software and similar programs.

Now that we've discussed what you need, let's consider what you don't. Take a look at your Desktop, the All Programs menu and even the Notification area to see what's showing there. See whether you can decipher what the program icons stand for and what the program is used for. Make a list of what you believe to be third-party programs. Now consider the following:

- Windows 7 comes with a music program (Windows Media Player), so there's no reason to keep third-party music-management programs that may be installed on your new laptop or netbook. Not only will these programs hog hard drive space, they will vie for control when you want to play media. Additionally, they may run in the background all the time, using system resources such as RAM. Beyond all of that, though, if you do need a third-party program it's most likely to be associated with hardware you own, such as a Zune or an iPod, and the third-party program installed now won't do you any good anyway.

- Manufacturers make deals with software makers to put software on your new computer that will work for 30, 60 or 90 days, then prompt you to buy it. They're betting that if they can get you hooked in that period, you'll shell out the money required to purchase the software when the trial expires. If you like the software and use it, you may be tempted to buy it. Perhaps that's OK; but perhaps it isn't. It may be slowing down your computer when a rival program would not. It may cost quite a bit of money when another program would do the same thing for free. You need to research this and get something that is both resource-friendly and inexpensive. Whatever the case, if you decide not to buy the trial software, you need to uninstall it.

- Windows 7 can burn DVDs. It can burn CDs. Windows 7 even has the option to burn disk images, and if you know what those are you also know that the software that does this can be quite expensive. Unless your computer has a specific program that etches the name of the program on the disk (Light Scribe technology), you can almost always get rid of that software, too.

How to clean up a new netbook or laptop (cont.)

Uninstalling an unwanted program

1 Click Start.

2 Click Control Panel.

3 Click Uninstall a program.

4 Select any program, toolbar or trial software to uninstall.

5 Click Uninstall.

■ Windows 7 has games. Most new computers come with games of their own. If you don't play games, don't like the games that came with your computer, or play only one specific game, uninstall the rest.

The point is this: go through the programs installed on your laptop or netbook and uninstall it. You do this from the Control Panel.

Programs
Uninstall a program   3

Uninstall or change a program

5 To uninstall a program, select it from the list and then click Uninstall, Change, or Repair.

Organize ▾   Uninstall   Change

Name	Publisher	Installed On	Siz
Apple Mobile Device Support	Apple Inc.	11/18/2010	
Apple Software Update	Apple Inc.	4/30/2010	
Audible Download Manager	Audible, Inc.	9/16/2010	
AudibleManager	Audible, Inc.	9/16/2010	
Bing Bar	Microsoft Corporation	9/30/2010	
BitPim 1.0.7	Joe Pham <djpham@bitpim.org>	6/21/2010	
Bonjour	Apple Inc.	11/18/2010	
Canon SELPHY CP770		5/10/2010	

4

Exploring the outside of laptops and netbooks

2

Introduction

Laptops and netbooks are much smaller than desktop PCs; you know that. But you may not know that the ports you have access to are basically the same. Like a desktop PC you'll probably have USB ports, an Ethernet port, and almost always an external monitor port. You'll probably also see a place to connect speakers or headphones. There might be a place to plug in a phone cord to access the Internet via dial-up or even a slot for inserting an SD card from a digital camera. If you have a laptop, you'll have a disk drive for viewing and/or burning CDs/DVDs, and perhaps even a FireWire port. You'll find laptop and netbook-related hardware too that you generally won't see on desktop PCs, such as a battery and battery bay, a button or slider for enabling and disabling Wi-Fi, and perhaps even built-in Bluetooth connectivity.

What you'll do

Locate and use the power cable

Locate and use USB ports

Locate and use sound ports

Locate and use a modem port

Locate and use Ethernet ports

Locate and use an external monitor port

Locate and use FireWire ports

Locate and use Bluetooth technology

Locate and insert or remove the battery

Explore basic hardware ▶

The best way to find out what's available on your laptop or netbook is to read the documentation that came with it. If you can't find a physical guide, there may be one installed on your computer. To find out, click Start, and in the Start Search window, type User Guide (or User's Guide). If you find one, click it in the Start menu results to open it.

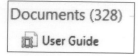

A User Guide will help you discover more about your computer. The User Guide will show what is available on the outside, detail specific features and offer tips for using the computer safely, among other things.

You can also find out what's installed using Device Manager or System Information, both included with Windows 7 but both equally cryptic when it comes to discovering what's physically installed on your computer. However you discover what is available on your laptop or netbook, even if it's simply looking at what's on the outside, you need to know what each of these ports looks like, what they do and how to use them. Device Manager is shown here, and the Network adapters section has been expanded so that you can see the network hardware installed on our netbook.

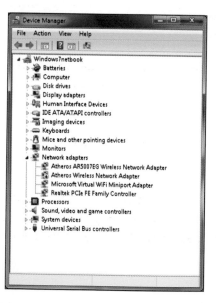

Did you know?

If a User Guide is not available, you can probably visit the manufacturer's website and download one.

26

The power cable

A power cable is the cable that you will use to connect the laptop to the wall outlet (power outlet). You can connect and disconnect the power cable at any time, even when the computer is running. When you connect the power cable to both the laptop and the power outlet, the laptop will use the power from the outlet and charge the battery at the same time. When you unplug the laptop from the power outlet, the laptop will run on stored battery power.

If you always use your laptop or netbook at home and it's always plugged in, you can remove the battery so that it does not continually charge itself. You can then insert the battery and charge it when you need to. This will lengthen the life of the battery because a battery can be charged only so many times and then can't be charged any more, thus with less use it will last longer. However, if you use the laptop or netbook a lot while it's running on battery power, leave the laptop plugged in when you can, that way the battery will always be fully charged when you need it.

USB ports

USB ports, or Universal Serial Bus ports, offer a place to connect USB devices. USB devices include mice, external keyboards, mobile phones, digital cameras and other devices, including USB flash drives. You may have a USB printer or scanner, for instance, or a USB flash drive you use for backing up data. USB cables don't always come with USB devices you purchase, so although you may have a USB device, unless you've purchased a USB cable separately, you may not have a USB cable.

The universal symbol for USB is shown here. Two USB ports are shown overleaf as well. The picture of the USB port was taken from my laptop's User Guide, and you may be able to find a similar User Guide with pictures on your laptop. USB ports are rectangular and small. Your laptop or netbook probably includes at least two of these ports, but it may have four or more.

Locating and using the power cable

2

1 Locate the power cord. It may consist of two pieces that need to be connected. One end will be small and will plug into the power port on your PC; the other end will plug into a wall outlet.

2 Connect the power cord to the back or side of the laptop as noted in the documentation. In almost all cases, there is only one port that a power cord can fit into. If it doesn't fit, it's not the right port. You may see a symbol similar to the one shown here.

3 Plug the power cord into the wall outlet.

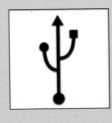

Explore basic hardware (cont.)

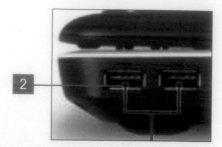

Locating and using USB ports

1. Locate a USB cable. It is sometimes rectangular on one end and almost square on the other. Both ends will probably look the same though, small and rectangular.

2. Plug the proper end of the USB cable into an empty USB port on your laptop. If it fits, it's the proper end.

3. Connect the other end to the USB device.

4. Often, though not always, you'll need to turn on the USB device so that Windows 7 recognises it. You do not generally have to 'turn on' USB storage units, such as flash drives.

5. Most of the time you can see USB devices in the Computer window. Just click Start, then Computer. Here, an empty USB flash drive is shown as Removable Disk (E:) on our laptop.

Sound ports

If there are any external sound ports, you'll probably see three. Most of the time you have access to a line-in jack, a microphone-in jack and a headphones/speaker/line-out jack. The symbols for these are shown here.

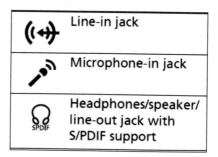

A line-in jack accepts audio from external devices, such as CD/DVD players. A microphone-in jack accepts input from external microphones. A headphone or speaker jack lets you connect your laptop to an external source for output, including but not limited to speakers and headphones.

Important !

Throughout this book we may use laptop or netbook or both to describe a portable computer. Unless specifically noted, the topic at hand refers to both.

Modems and Ethernet

A modem port lets you connect your laptop or netbook to a phone jack using a standard telephone cord. Once connected, you can connect to the Internet using a dial-up connection, provided you've signed up for a dial-up Internet subscription. The telephone cable must be connected to both the wall and the laptop. Here's the universal symbol for a dial-up modem.

Did you know? ?

Ethernet is faster than Wi-Fi. When you have the ability to connect to either, such as when you are working at home and near an Ethernet device (router, switch, hub), choose Ethernet for best performance.

Explore basic hardware (cont.)

Locating and using sound ports

2

1 If necessary, plug the device into an electrical outlet (speakers) or insert batteries (portable music players).

2 If necessary, turn on the device.

3 Insert the cables that connect the device to the laptop or netbook in the proper port. Remember, line-in jacks bring data into the laptop; line-out jacks port data out to external devices such as speakers or headphones.

4 If prompted, work through any set-up processes.

Locating and using a modem port

1 Connect the laptop to a phone jack using a telephone cord.

2 Connect using your dial-up Internet connection.

Explore basic hardware (cont.)

Locating and using Ethernet ports

1 Locate an Ethernet cable.

2 Connect the cable to both the PC and the Ethernet outlet on a router or cable modem (or a wall in a hotel).

3 Most of the time, you'll see that a network is available in the Notification area of the Taskbar. Click it to join.

4 When prompted, click Home, Work or Public, as applicable.

See also

Chapters 5 and 6 discuss joining networks at length.

Ethernet, also called RJ-45, is used to connect a computer to a local, wired network. If you have a cable modem, router or other high-speed Internet device at home, you'll probably use Ethernet to connect to it. If you want to connect to a hotel network, you may use Ethernet to do that, too. An Ethernet cable looks like a telephone cable, except both ends are slightly larger. Both ends of an Ethernet cable are always the same, though, which is unlike some of the other cables we've discussed so far. The universal symbol for Ethernet is shown here. When looking for an Ethernet port on your laptop or netbook, look for this symbol and/or an almost square port. The Ethernet cable will snap in.

Important

When travelling, always take your own Ethernet cable. Most hotels don't loan them out.

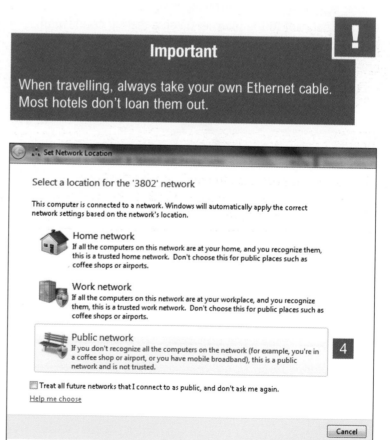

Set Network Location

Select a location for the '3802' network

This computer is connected to a network. Windows will automatically apply the correct network settings based on the network's location.

Home network
If all the computers on this network are at your home, and you recognize them, this is a trusted home network. Don't choose this for public places such as coffee shops or airports.

Work network
If all the computers on this network are at your workplace, and you recognize them, this is a trusted work network. Don't choose this for public places such as coffee shops or airports.

Public network
If you don't recognize all the computers on the network (for example, you're in a coffee shop or airport, or you have mobile broadband), this is a public network and is not trusted.

4

☐ Treat all future networks that I connect to as public, and don't ask me again.

Help me choose

Cancel

External monitor port

Most portable computers come with an external monitor port, although you may occasionally come across a very small netbook that doesn't have one. With this port you can connect your computer to a secondary monitor or network projector where you can mirror what you see on the laptop's screen or extend the screen to the second monitor. The universal symbol for an external display (VGA) port is shown here, as is the actual 15-pin VGA port.

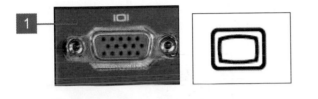

For your information

If you are not prompted to configure the display as shown here, press and hold the Windows key and press P. (We always figured that 'P' stood for 'projector'.)

Locating and using an external monitor port

2

1. Locate a port on your laptop that is in the shape of a trapezoid and contains 15 pin holes. Look for this icon.

2. Connect a VGA display to this port using the cable attached to the display.

3. Plug in and turn on the display.

4. When prompted, select how to use the display. Computer only is the default, and you can click Duplicate, Extend or Projector only as desired.

Locating and using your Wi-Fi button

▶

?

Did you know?

Your computer can't join a Wi-Fi network if Wi-Fi is disabled on your computer.

Almost all laptops and netbooks have some sort of button or slider on the outside of the computer that enables you to quickly enable and disable Wi-Fi. The reason this is so important is that when Wi-Fi is enabled, your computer constantly searches for a Wi-Fi network to join. This constant search drains your battery faster than if the device was not looking for such a connection. If you're out and about, perhaps heading to the local library or Internet café, you'll want this to be enabled. If you're at home, connected to your Ethernet network, or somewhere that a Wi-Fi network is not available (such as a cabin in the woods), it does not need to be enabled. Look around on the outside of your computer for a slider or button with the Wi-Fi logo on it. Here are a few variations of this.

Almost all computers these days come with a slot for inserting some sort of memory card. There are several variations, but the SD card seems to be the most popular right now. Look on the outside of your laptop or netbook for a small slot, about 1 inch long. If you find one, see whether you can insert a memory card. Once you insert the card, you'll get a pop-up like this one, prompting you about what you'd like to do with it.

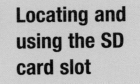

Locating and using the SD card slot

Important

You won't see the option to import pictures if there aren't any pictures on the SD card!

AutoPlay window:

SD/MMC (D:)

☐ Always do this for pictures:

Pictures options

Import pictures and videos
using Windows

Import pictures and videos
using Windows Live Photo Gallery

View pictures
using Windows Live Photo Gallery

General options

Open folder to view files
using Windows Explorer

Use this drive for backup
using Windows Backup

Speed up my system
using Windows ReadyBoost

View more AutoPlay options in Control Panel

Explore hardware generally found only on laptops

Locating and using FireWire ports

1 Locate your FireWire cable.

2 Plug the appropriate end of the cable into the FireWire device.

3 Plug the other end of the cable into the FireWire port on the laptop. (Not many netbooks have this port.)

4 Often, you'll have to turn on the FireWire device for Windows 7 to recognise it.

There are two items that are generally offered on laptops only (and not netbooks). They are FireWire ports and CD/DVD drives.

FireWire, also called IEEE 1394, is often used to connect digital video cameras, professional audio hardware and external hard drives to a computer. FireWire connections are much faster than USB and are better than anything else when you need to transfer large amounts of data, such as digital video. FireWire ports are generally not available on netbooks because they don't have the necessary computing power to transfer the data and work with it. Editing and storing large video files, for instance, takes quite a bit of computer resources.

Unlike USB devices, many devices that require a FireWire cable often come with one. When searching for a FireWire port on your newer laptop, look for an extremely small, rectangular port, with the numbers 1394 beside it, or a symbol similar to the one shown here. On an older laptop, the FireWire port may be larger, but often these larger FireWire ports are used only on older desktop PCs.

Important !

Not all laptops come with a FireWire port.

CD/DVD drives enable you to insert physical CDs and DVDs for the purpose of installing software, watching movies and transferring data stored on them. You'll know if you have a drive like this by looking on the outside. To open the drive, simply press the button on it.

If you don't have a CD/DVD drive and need to install software, you still can. The instructions for doing that are laid out in Chapter 14.

If you've seen people talking on their mobile phones using a headset (while leaving their phones in their pocket or bag), you've seen Bluetooth technology in action. Bluetooth is used to create 'personal' networks, to connect devices that are in close range. A laptop or netbook may come with built-in Bluetooth capabilities (although this is not very common), or you can add it by purchasing and installing a USB Bluetooth *dongle*. A Bluetooth dongle is a small device, about the size of a USB flash drive, that connects directly to a USB port on the outside of the portable computer.

Once a Bluetooth dongle is installed, Bluetooth connections can be made between your laptop and any of the following Bluetooth-enabled devices (and this is not a complete list): mobile phones, other laptops and netbooks, PCs, printers, GPS receivers, digital cameras and game consoles. The universal symbol for Bluetooth is shown here. As with Wi-Fi, it's best to leave Bluetooth disabled until you need it. When it's enabled it's constantly looking for Bluetooth devices to connect to, which drains battery power.

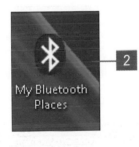

! Important

Bluetooth is best used when the two devices are close together and very little data needs to be transferred (as is the case with a mouse and its Bluetooth dongle).

You know your portable computer has a battery. What you may not know is that there are several components that are to do with the battery. There's often a battery lock, a battery bay and the battery itself.

Bluetooth and batteries

Locating and using Bluetooth technology

2

1 If necessary, insert the Bluetooth dongle and install any drivers required.

2 On the portable computer, click My Bluetooth Places, or whatever icon represents the Bluetooth device you have installed.

3 Turn on the external Bluetooth device.

4 Work through the set-up wizard as prompted.

Bluetooth and batteries (cont.)

Locating and inserting or removing the battery

1. Turn off the laptop or netbook properly, using Start and Shut Down.

2. Unplug the laptop from the wall outlet and remove the power cable. Set the power cable aside.

3. Carefully turn the laptop upside down and place it on a desk or table.

4. Locate the battery bay and open it.

5. Unlatch the battery latch.

6. Remove or install the battery.

7. Lock the battery into place.

8. Secure the latch.

9. Close the battery bay door.

Did you know?

You can purchase an 'extended life' battery so that you can run your computer longer without having to recharge it or plug it in. These batteries cost more than regular-life batteries and are larger and heavier, which may not be acceptable to you. The advantages outweigh the disadvantages for us, though, and they may for you, too.

The battery components are generally on the bottom of the portable computer. Thus, before you turn the laptop or netbook upside down to look at it, make sure you turn off the laptop and unplug it.

You'll probably find the following items on the back of the laptop, at least regarding the battery:

- Battery bay – this holds the computer battery. Sometimes you have to use a screwdriver to get inside the battery bay, other times you simply need to slide out the compartment door.

- Battery release latch – this latch holds the battery in place, even after the battery bay's door has been opened. You'll need to release this latch to get to the battery.

- Battery lock – this locks the battery in position.

Exploring the inside

3

Introduction

When you open your laptop or netbook for the first time, you'll probably be able to find the power button, keyboard keys, touchpad and display screen, but you can be sure there are plenty of hidden features. There may be a microphone, web cam, speakers and 'easy-launch' buttons, for starters. To get the most out of your portable computer you should be aware of all of the features, and if configurable, personalise them.

Your portable computer is probably not the same make and model as mine, nor is it the same as other readers' models, so this chapter may seem a bit generic. All laptops and netbooks do have display screens, keyboards, arrow keys, specialised keys and Function keys, though, so we have a pretty good starting point. Some portable computers have buttons that you can configure, too, buttons that will open, with a single click, your email application, web browser, music program, or favourite application. We'll look at all of this here, starting with basic functionality.

What you'll do

Locate the power button and speakers

Locate the microphone

Locate the web camera

Use the touchpad

Use common keys

Use the arrow keys

Use the Function keys

> **!**
> ## Important
>
> The best way to find out what's available inside your laptop or netbook is to read the documentation that came with it, as noted in Chapter 2. If a User Guide is not available (either on your computer or in printed form in the box it came in), you can probably visit the manufacturer's website and download one.

Basic functionality ▶

Some features are included in all portable computers. There's always some sort of a latch for opening the laptop or netbook's lid, a power button for turning it on, some sort of pointing device (often a touchpad) and, of course, the display. There may also be a microphone or webcam. Let's find them.

Power and sound

The first thing you'll want to discover, of course, is the power button. You press the power button to 'boot' the computer (start it up) so that you can use it. The computer has to complete several boot-up tasks, including checking to see that internal hardware such as RAM is available and functional, loading the operating system, checking for a display and more. Once that's done, you should hear the familiar 'welcome' tone.

If you hear a welcome sound when the computer has finished these tasks, you will know that your computer's speakers are working properly. If you don't hear anything but a single beep, your audio features are disabled or aren't functioning properly. Most of the time, though, you'll hear that welcome sound, even if the sound you hear is too loud or too soft and requires tweaking. The point is that right after booting is a great time to adjust the sound level.

Locating the power button and speakers

1 Locate the latch on the outside of the laptop or netbook to open the lid.

2 Locate the power button. It may have the universal power button symbol on it. Press it to boot the computer.

3 Watch the computer's progress on the display screen.

4 When the computer has finished its startup tasks, look to the bottom of the display screen. Locate the Volume icon in the Notification area.

5 Click the Volume icon once.

6 Use the slider to increase or decrease the volume.

7 Follow the sound to locate the speakers.

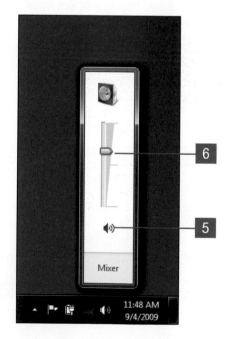

Microphone and web camera

All of the laptops and netbooks we've seen also offer a microphone and a webcam. You'll use these to video chat with others over the Internet. Chapter 11 outlines how to do this, because you'll not only need a working microphone and webcam, you'll also need to obtain some program for communicating through them. Before you get to that chapter, though, you'll want to make sure you have the required hardware components. If they are there and disabled, you'll need to enable them. Chances are that none of this is necessary, but for the purpose of being thorough, it's best to double-check.

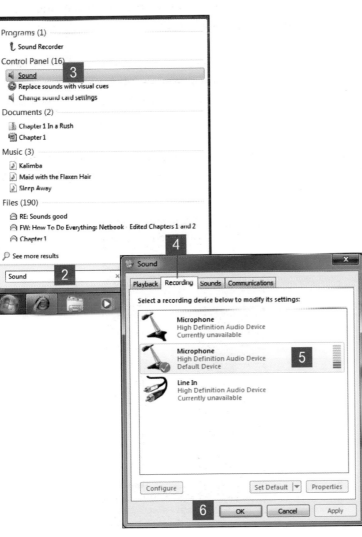

Basic functionality (cont.)

Locating the microphone

1 Click Start.

2 In the Start Search window, type Sound.

3 In the results list, under Control Panel, click Sound.

4 Click the Recording tab.

5 Locate a working microphone. Here, one microphone is active.

6 Click OK.

3

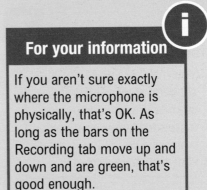

For your information

If you aren't sure exactly where the microphone is physically, that's OK. As long as the bars on the Recording tab move up and down and are green, that's good enough.

Locating the web camera ▶

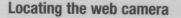

Locating the web camera

1 Look for a small camera eye, which should be located at the top of the display. This is the webcam.

2 Click Start.

3 In the Start Search window, type Devices.

4 In the results, under Control Panel, click Devices and Printers.

5 If a webcam is installed, you'll find it in the Devices and Printers window.

For your information

You may or may not see a webcam lens and/or a webcam may not be included with your laptop. To find out, complete steps 2–5.

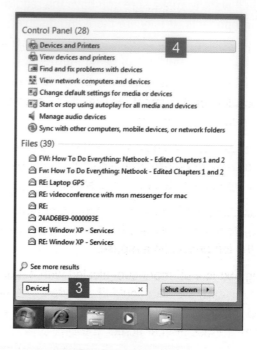

?

Did you know?

You may be able to double-click the webcam icon to start it. However, you need a program to communicate with your contacts via video chat over the Internet.

The keyboard, of course, enables you to type commands, navigate windows and access various parts of programs and the operating system windows. You'll learn quite a bit about the keyboard shortly.

The touchpad is the computer's 'mouse' and enables you to move the cursor around on the screen. Like a mouse, it often also offers a left and right mouse 'key'. These buttons do the same thing that left and right buttons on a mouse do.

Here are a few things to consider regarding the touchpad:

- Tapping is a common way to place the cursor somewhere, open a window or document, or execute a command. You can single-tap or double-tap.

- Touching and then dragging your finger on the touchpad is a common way to reposition the cursor on the page. (You can then tap to apply the position, say in a line of text.)

- Double-clicking is often used to open a program, document, file or window. Generally, the left button functions the same way as the left button on a mouse.

- Selecting text is a bit more complicated with a touchpad. Position the cursor where you'd like to start selecting text, click and hold the left touchpad's button and use your finger to drag the mouse pointer across the desired text.

- Right-clicking is a common way to open contextual menus to access commands such as Copy and Select All. The right button functions the same way as the right button of a mouse.

- Using the middle button, if one exists, is often a way to scroll through web pages or windows that are longer than one page.

Using the touchpad and the keyboard

!

Important

Throughout this book when you see the word 'click' it means to tap once.

3

?

Did you know?

If you have trouble using the touchpad, consider a small USB mouse. Manufacturers make these specifically for laptops and netbooks and they fit easily in a laptop/netbook bag or a handbag. We always connect a mouse to our laptops and netbooks, simply because we feel it makes them easier to use.

Using the touchpad and the keyboard (cont.)

Using the touchpad

1 Place your finger on the touchpad and move it around. Notice the mouse moves.

2 Double-tap the touchpad with the cursor positioned over any document or file to open it.

3 Move the cursor to any place on a page that contains text. Tap once to place the cursor there.

4 Hold down the left button on the touchpad and drag your finger across any text to select it.

5 Click the right touchpad button to see the 'contextual' menus, such as Copy and Paste (while text is selected).

6 If there is a centre button, try clicking and holding it to move up, down, left or right on a page.

Joli Ballew ✕ Search

About 32,300 results (0.24 seconds) Advanced search

▸ **Joli Ballew** 🔍
Welcome, I am **Joli Ballew**, a Microsoft MVP (Desktop Experience), a technology trainer, and writer in the Dallas area. I hold several certifications ...
www.**joliballew**.com/ - Cached - Similar

Previous Columns by **Joli Ballew** 🔍
Joli Ballew is a technology trainer and writer in the Dallas area. She holds several certifications including MCSE, A+, and MCDST. In addition to writing, ...
www.microsoft.com › Expert Zone › Meet the Experts - Cached - Similar

Important !

Make sure your fingers and hands are clean when using the touchpad – it has a sensitive surface.

Most laptop keyboards have more than a few universal keys, and much of the time these keys offer the same things across makes and models. For instance, pressing F1 almost always opens a Help window for the open application. The Windows key opens the Start menu, and the Windows key in combination with other keys will do other things, such as minimise all windows (Start + M) or lock your computer (Start + L). The Caps Lock key makes sure anything you type appears in capital letters only, and the Num Lock key makes sure your number pad offers numbers and nothing else.

There are arrow keys, too, which you can use to move around in a web page, document or other window. Page Up and Page Down keys let you move around as well. And there are always Function keys, which offer shortcuts to specific computer-related functions, most of which are make and model specific.

Did you know?

The Taskbar is the transparent bar that runs across the bottom of the display screen and the Internet Explorer button looks like a big, blue E.

There are literally hundreds of keyboard shortcuts, and my goal in this chapter does not include listing them or suggesting you learn them. However, the Windows Start key, also called the Windows Logo key, can be a real time saver if you can get in the habit of using it regularly. That said, here are a few shortcuts you can commit to memory:

- Windows Logo key – open the Start menu.

- Windows Logo key + E – open My Computer.

- Windows Logo key + D – Show Desktop (and minimise all open windows).

- Windows Logo key + M – minimise all windows.

- Windows Logo key + L – switch between users or lock the laptop.

Keys common to most keyboards

Using common keys

1. Click the Windows Logo key to open the Start menu.
2. Click the Windows Logo key (which I'll call the Start key from here on) to close the Start menu.
3. Click the Start key + E to open Computer.
4. Click the Start key + F to open a search window.
5. Click the Start key + F1 to open Help and Support.
6. Click the Start key + D to show the Desktop.
7. Click the Start key + Shift + M to maximise all minimised windows.
8. Click the X at the top of each open window to close it.

Keys common to most keyboards (cont.)

9 Locate the button for Internet Explorer on the Taskbar and tap it once.

10 Click Ctrl + T to open a new tab (where you can type an Internet address).

11 Click Shift + F10 to open a context menu you'd normally get by right-clicking inside Internet Explorer.

12 Close Internet Explorer.

- Windows Logo key + F – open Search.
- Windows Logo key + F1 – open Help and Support.

The Ctrl (Control) key rarely does anything by itself, but when pressed with other keys, it becomes active. Ctrl + Alt + Del opens a new screen where you can lock the computer, switch users, log off, change a password, or start Task Manager, for instance. Here are a few options you may want to explore:

- Ctrl + O – opens the Open window where you can search for and open a file, folder or program.
- Ctrl + P – opens the Print dialogue box.
- Ctrl + S – saves the current document.
- Ctrl + T – opens a new tab in Internet Explorer.
- Esc – stops the current activity, usually.
- Tab – advances the cursor to the next tab stop.

Shift, like the Ctrl key, generally does nothing by itself, but when used with other keys, it performs tasks. Here are a few options you may want to explore:

- Shift + F10 – opens a contextual menu you'd normally get by right-clicking.
- Shift + Delete – deletes the selected item permanently.
- Shift + any letter – in a word document, capitalises the letter you type.
- Home/End – Home moves the cursor to the beginning of a paragraph, line or document, depending on the current placement of the cursor. End moves to the end of the paragraph, line or document.

Fn, like Shift and Ctrl, doesn't do anything by itself but instead is used to access items listed on the F1, F2, F3, etc. buttons. The items listed are laptop specific and may offer options to change the volume, lock the laptop, put the laptop to sleep, set number lock or scroll lock, and more.

Scroll lock's use varies, depending on the application open, but is rarely used on today's laptops.

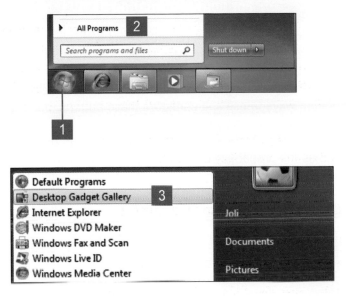

Using the arrow keys

1 Click Start.

2 Click All Programs.

3 Click (tap) Desktop Gadget Gallery to open it.

4 Use the arrow keys on the keyboard to move through the gadgets.

5 Click the X in the top right corner of the Gadget Gallery to close it.

Using the Function keys

1 Locate the Fn key on your keyboard. If you do not see an Fn key, read the second 'Did you know?' note here.

2 Notice the colour of the text or images under F1, F2, F3 and other function keys. It may be blue, green or any colour other than the colour of the keyboard letters. Under F1 you may see a blue question mark, for instance. This alternate-coloured information tells you what will happen when you press the Fn key and this key at the same time.

Did you know?

A 'gadget' is a small program icon you can drag to your Desktop for up-to-date information on things such as the weather, the time or the news.

Did you know?

Although most laptops and netbooks offer an Fn key, some do not. If you don't see an Fn key, take a look at the items listed underneath F1, F2, F3, F4 and so on. They will probably be a different colour than default keys on the keyboard. Locate a key that is the same colour as this one, a key that has an F on it or something similar. This is most likely the Fn key we're talking about here.

Keys common to most keyboards (cont.)

3 Press Fn + F1. This will generally open Help.

4 Press Fn + F2. Make a note of what happens as well as what is listed under F2 on the key itself.

5 Continue in this manner until you've explored all the function keys, up to F12. (Some keys may not do anything.)

6 Look for other keys on the keyboard that have additional information on them other than letters or punctuation. For instance, you may see additional functionality on the arrow keys (which is where you might access the volume or brightness), or on the Page Up and Page Down keys (where you may find options to scroll left or right). Explore these keys.

For your information

All of the laptops I've seen recently come with specialised buttons that you can configure. These often include buttons for Mail, Web Browser, Bluetooth or Music Player, among others. Each manufacturer offers different ways to use and configure these buttons, so you'll need to access your user guide to find out exactly how to do this. For the most part, all you need to do is press the proper key on the keyboard and follow the configuration directions, or access the Keyboard option in Control Panel to configure the available buttons.

Getting started with Windows 7

Introduction

You read through a brief introduction to netbooks, laptops and Windows 7 in Chapter 1, and you explored the outside and the inside of your laptop or netbook in Chapters 2 and 3. Now it's time to dig a little deeper into Windows 7, exploring the Desktop, Taskbar, Notification area, applications, accessories, and how to personalise Windows 7 to best meet your needs. You'll also want to know how to best use the Windows default folders and libraries, and what your options are for shutting down Windows 7 safely. First, though, you'll want to find out what edition of Windows 7 you have – each edition offers varying degrees of features.

What you'll do

Know your Windows 7 edition

Explore the Desktop

Add Desktop icons

Add a gadget to the Desktop

Explore the Taskbar and Notification area

Discover Windows 7 applications

Discover Windows 7 accessories

Select a new background and screensaver

Change the screen resolution

Explore Windows 7's folder structure

Create a search folder

Shut down Windows

Know your Windows 7 edition

▶

You may or may not know what edition of Windows 7 is installed on your laptop or netbook. If you're using a bare-bones netbook, it may be Windows 7 Starter. If you're using a high-end laptop, perhaps it's Windows 7 Professional. You can find out what edition you have from the System window. Our netbook is running Windows 7 Home Premium. It came with Windows 7 Starter, but we upgraded using Windows Anytime Upgrade shortly after purchasing it.

> View basic information about your computer
>
> Windows edition
>
> Windows 7 Home Premium
>
> Copyright © 2009 Microsoft Corporation. All rights reserved.
>
> Get more features with a new edition of Windows 7

Although Microsoft offers various editions to meet the needs of users worldwide, the editions built specifically for consumers are:

- Windows 7 Starter – this edition contains the fewest features. It does have many of the features you'll see outlined in this book, though, including jump lists, the ability to pin items to the Taskbar and the Start menu, Windows Search, the ability to join home and public Wi-Fi networks and install hardware, and it comes with programs such as Internet Explorer 8. It has limitations, however: you can't create a homegroup, play a DVD, or change the Desktop background. It doesn't support Aero, which means you can't use the 'peek' or Taskbar 'previews', and you can't switch users without completely logging off. However, if you just need the basics, this will do.

- Windows 7 Home Premium – this edition was created for the home user and contains all the Starter features and more. It offers all the Windows 7 features you need, a full-function PC experience, and is a visually rich environment. This edition comes with Media Player, Media Center, Internet Explorer 8, the Action Center, DeviceStage, and accessories including the Calculator, Notepad, Paint,

Sync Center and more. The key features are Aero Glass, Aero Background, Windows Touch, the ability to create a homegroup, Media Center, DVD playback and authoring, and premium games.

- Windows 7 Professional – this edition was created for small businesses and for people who work at home. It offers business-related tools along with the applications you'll need to function in a business environment where security and productivity are critical. Key features are the ability to join a corporate domain, Remote Desktop host, location-aware printing, Encrypting File System, Mobility Center, Presentation Mode and Offline Folders.

- Windows 7 Ultimate – this is the 'ultimate' version and contains all the available features. Key features include the ability to switch among 35 languages, protect data with BitLocker encryption, and more. You probably can't upgrade a small netbook to Windows 7 Ultimate because it may lack the required resources.

Did you know?

There are other versions of Windows 7 you may hear about, but they are geared towards large corporations (Windows 7 Enterprise) and emerging countries (Windows 7 Basic).

Knowing your Windows 7 edition

1 Click the Start button.

2 Right-click Computer.

3 Click Properties.

4 Read the system information. You'll see your Windows edition at the top of the window (as shown on page 50), and information about your PC's processor, RAM, system type, computer name, workgroup name and activation information underneath (shown overleaf).

4

Know your Windows 7 edition (cont.)

System	
Rating:	**2.3** Windows Experience Index
Processor:	Intel(R) Atom(TM) CPU N270 @ 1.60GHz 1.60 GHz
Installed memory (RAM):	1.00 GB
System type:	32-bit Operating System
Pen and Touch:	No Pen or Touch Input is available for this Display

Computer name, domain, and workgroup settings	
Computer name:	Windows7netbook
Full computer name:	Windows7netbook
Computer description:	
Workgroup:	WORKGROUP

Windows activation	
Windows is activated	

Did you know?

You can click Windows Experience Index to rate and see how you can improve your computer's performance. Tips for improving performance include adjusting visual effects, using Disk Cleanup, adjusting power settings, and more.

Jargon buster

Processor – short for microprocessor, it's the silicon chip that contains the central processing unit (CPU) inside a computer. Generally, the terms CPU and processor are used interchangeably. A CPU does almost all of the computer's calculations and is the most important piece of hardware in a computer system.

RAM – short for random access memory, it's the hardware inside your computer that temporarily stores data that is being used by the operating system or programs. Although there are many types of RAM, all you need to know is that the more RAM you have, the faster your computer will (theoretically) run and perform. It's often hard to add physical RAM to a netbook, but you can enhance performance with Ready Boost (detailed in Chapter 13).

System type – you'll have either a 32-bit or a 64-bit operating system. Stating the difference would require a few pages of explanation, but suffice it to say that 64-bit computers are faster than 32-bit computers because they can process more data, more quickly.

What you see on the Desktop will vary depending on how long you've been using your computer, its Windows 7 edition, and what manufacturer created it. If it's brand new, you may see only the Recycle Bin. If you've been using Windows 7 for a while, you may see other things, including Computer, Network, Control Panel, or a folder with your name on it (for storing your personal files). You may even see icons with names of applications or Internet service providers written on them. If you've worked with gadgets, you may have those, too. Here is a sample Desktop.

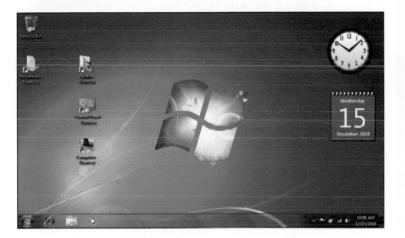

Here are a few of the things you may find on your Desktop:

- Recycle Bin – this holds deleted files until you decide to empty it. The Recycle Bin serves as a safeguard, allowing you to recover items you have accidentally deleted, or items you thought you no longer wanted but later decide you need. Note that once you empty the Recycle Bin, the items in it are gone for ever. (You can empty the Recycle Bin by right-clicking it and choosing Empty Recycle Bin.)

Explore the Desktop (cont.)

■ Gadgets – these are desktop components you manually select from the Desktop Gadget Gallery. The gallery includes several gadgets you can add to the Desktop, including but not limited to a calendar, clock, currency converter, picture puzzle and up-to-the-minute weather information.

■ Computer – double-clicking this icon opens the Computer window, shown here. (You can also click Computer from the Start menu.) You can see your hard disk drive(s) where the operating system, installed applications and personal data are stored, along with CD or DVD drives (if they exist). Note on this netbook, there's only one drive, the hard drive, and no external drives.

■ Your personal folder – the name of this folder is the user name you created when you set up Windows 7. Every user account has a personal folder. Inside this folder are subfolders named My Documents, My Music, My Pictures, Downloads, Searches, My Videos and more. You'll use these folders to store your personal data.

Besides the icons that are on the desktop now, there are Windows 7 icons you can add or remove. You can choose to view or hide Computer, Recycle Bin, Control Panel, Network and your personal user folder.

Exploring the Desktop

1 If any windows are open, minimise or close them.

2 Locate the Recycle Bin.

3 Notice any other icons, including Network or Computer, or your personal file folder (the one with your name on it).

4 Locate the Start button. It's on the bottom left corner of the Taskbar.

5 Locate the clock and volume on the Taskbar's Notification area. (You may see additional icons.)

6 Locate any gadget on the Desktop.

7 Locate application icons to the right of the Start button.

4

Explore the
Desktop (cont.)

Control Panel Home

Change desktop icons   3
Change mouse pointers
Change your account picture

Adding Desktop icons

1. Right-click an empty area of the Desktop.

2. Click Personalize.

3. Click Change desktop icons.

4. Select the icons you want to appear on your Desktop.

5. Click OK.

Did you know?

If you have more than one user account on your computer, each user can configure their Desktop as they wish.

You can also choose to add shortcuts to programs you use often. You may want to add shortcuts to the Desktop for folders you create, programs you use often, or network places, such as folders stored on other computers. You can even add a shortcut to a public folder, or a single file or picture.

If you opt to put shortcuts to personal files and folders on your Desktop, note that there are several ways to do it. For a program, the easiest way is to click Start and locate the item for which you want to create a shortcut. Then, right-click it and drag it to the Desktop and click Create Shortcuts Here. For personal data you can right-click the file or folder, click Send to and then Desktop (create shortcut).

Adding a gadget to the Desktop

1 Click Start.

2 Click All Programs.

3 Click Desktop Gadget Gallery.

4 Drag any gadget to the Desktop.

5 Hover your mouse over the new gadget and click the wrench icon.

6 Configure the options as desired.

4

Explore the Desktop (cont.)

The Taskbar is the transparent bar that runs across the bottom of the screen and contains icons you've pinned there, open programs, the Start button and the Notification area. You can configure the Taskbar's properties by right-clicking it and clicking Properties. Take a look at what's on your computer's Taskbar.

Exploring the Taskbar and Notification area

1 Click Start and click All Programs.

2 Open several programs.

3 Click Start and click Pictures.

4 Click Start and click Documents.

5 Note the icons on the Taskbar.

6 Hover your mouse over any item to see its thumbnail. (We've minimised everything on our screen so you can see the thumbnail better.)

7 Hover your mouse over each icon at the far right area of the Taskbar – this is the Notification area.

8 Click the arrow to see hidden icons.

Important

You will not have access to all the features outlined in this chapter (or book) if you use Windows 7 Starter.

Important

What you see in the Notification area is running in the background and using system resources. If you see unwanted programs running, right-click and select Close or Exit.

Just about anything you want to access on your computer can be accessed through the Start menu. You can access office applications, graphics applications, games, even your personal folders. You can access Computer, Help and Support, and Control Panel, too. In this section, though, we'll look at only one part of the Start menu – the All Programs menu. It's important to note that Windows 7 Starter is missing some of these programs (such as Windows DVD Maker) and other editions may have limited functionality on a lower-end netbook or laptop (Windows Media Center, for instance). However, it's best to cover our bases and who knows, you may want to use Windows Anytime Upgrade to move up one edition to get more features (provided you have an upgradable netbook or laptop).

■ Internet Explorer 8 – one software option for accessing and surfing the Web. Internet Explorer offers tabbed browsing, meaning you can have several web pages open at the same time, a place to store links to your favourite pages, a pop-up blocker, and the ability to zoom, change the text size, print, and subscribe to RSS feeds, among other things. You'll learn more about Internet Explorer in Chapter 7.

■ Windows Media Player – an application that enables you to store, access, play and organise the music stored on your computer. You can also 'rip' music (that means copying music CDs you own to your hard drive), burn CDs, sync portable devices, and more. Media Player is covered in Chapter 12.

■ Windows DVD Maker – an application that lets you create DVDs easily by working through a series of steps, offered by the Windows DVD Maker wizard.

■ Windows Update – an application that allows you to manually or automatically obtain and install updates to your computer to keep it secure.

■ Windows Media Center – an application that allows you to watch, record, fast-forward and (after recording or pausing a TV show) rewind live TV, provided your computer includes the required hardware and resources. You can also listen to music stored on your computer, locate and watch sports programmes, view, download and/or purchase online

◀ **Discover Windows 7 applications**

4

media, burn CDs and DVDs (if your computer includes a CD/DVD drive), sync portable music devices, view and organise your personal pictures and videos, and more. To have access to all of Media Center's features you'll need a TV tuner, CD and DVD burner, Internet connection, large hard drive and lots of RAM.

■ Games – available from the Start menu, you can choose from all kinds of games, including Chess Titans, Internet Checkers and Solitaire.

Important

The applications introduced here are not all the applications that come with Windows 7. There are many we did not list in the interest of time, space and importance, or because the features are better introduced independently in other chapters.

Discovering Windows 7 applications

1 Click the Start button.

2 Click All Programs.

3 If necessary, use the scroll bar to move to the top of the All Programs list.

4 Locate Internet Explorer.

5 Continue down the list, noting what programs and applications are available in your edition of Windows 7.

Windows 7 also comes with a lot of accessories. These are applications, but they are simpler than the applications introduced thus far. Two examples are the Calculator and Notepad. Accessories are located in the Accessories folder, which you can access from the Start button and the All Programs list.

Accessories in the Accessories folder you may be interested in include:

- Calculator – a standard calculator you can use to perform basic mathematical tasks.

- Command Prompt – a command prompt that you can use to communicate with Windows 7's operating system, a task you'll probably never need.

Discover Windows 7 applications (cont.)

■ Connect to a Projector – a quick way to connect to a projector when giving a presentation.

■ Notepad – an application that enables you to type notes and save them. With this application you can also print, cut, copy and paste, find and replace words, and select a font, font size and script.

■ Paint – a program you can use to create drawings either on a blank canvas or on top of a picture. You can use the toolbar to draw shapes, lines, curves, and input text. You can use additional tools, including paintbrushes, pencils, airbrushes and the like, as well as choose colours for objects you draw.

■ Run – a dialogue box where you can type a command. There are many commands – sfc/scannow will cause Windows 7 to find and fix problems with the operating system; msconfig opens a dialogue box where you can control which programs load when you start Windows.

■ Snipping Tool – a tool you can use to copy any part of any screen, including information from a web page, part of your Desktop, or even part of a picture.

■ Sound Recorder – a recording program you can use to record your own voice. You can use the voice clips as reminders for tasks and you can add them to Movie Maker files or a web page, among other things.

■ Sync Center – a feature of Windows that allows you to keep information in sync between your computer and network servers and certain mobile devices. These devices may include music players, phones and even digital cameras.

■ Windows Explorer – a way to open an 'explorer' window where you can browse for files, programs, pictures, music, videos and more. It's generally easier to locate these items in their respective folders or from the Start menu.

■ Windows Mobility Center – a way to access the tools often required by laptop and netbook users. Mobility Center is where you can quickly mute the volume, view battery status and change battery plans, turn Wi-Fi features off or on, connect a display, or set up a sync partnership.

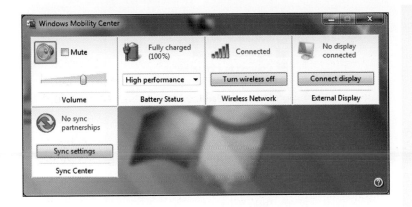

■ WordPad – a word-processing program where you can create, edit, save and print files. Like Notepad, you can cut, copy and paste, find and replace words, and select a font, font size and script. However, you also have access to a formatting toolbar, a ruler and additional options. You can insert the date and time into a document, and an object, such as a graph or chart, or a compatible picture.

There are some other folders available inside the Accessories folder. Subfolders you may be interested in include:

■ Ease of Access folder – allows you to access tools that make using the computer easier for those with disabilities. Items include a magnifier and narrator.

■ System Tools – allows you to access tools you'll need to maintain your computer's health. These include but are not limited to Disk Cleanup, Disk Defragmenter and System Restore.

■ Tablet PC – enables you to access tools related to mobile PCs, such as the Tablet PC input panel and Windows Journal, among other things.

Discover Windows 7 applications (cont.)

Discovering Windows 7 accessories

1. Click the Start button, then All Programs.

2. Use the scroll bar to move down the list until you see Accessories.

3. Click Accessories.

4. Click Calculator.

5. Repeat steps 1–4 and click Paint.

6. Repeat steps 1–4 and click Sound Recorder.

7. Continue as desired, exploring additional features.

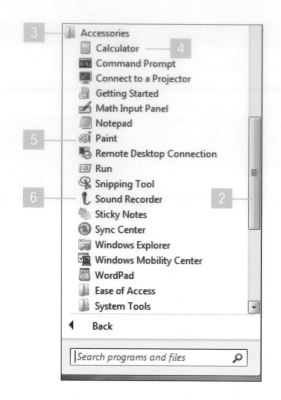

You can personalise Windows 7 in lots of ways, by changing the Desktop background, applying a theme, applying a screensaver, even changing the screen resolution, among other things. You do all of these things from the Personalization window in Control Panel. Some of this is cosmetic, but other things, such as screen resolution, can enhance how you use the computer by making items on the screen easier to see.

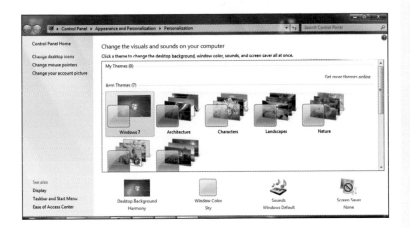

One of the things you'll probably want to change is the background. The background is the picture you see on the Desktop when no windows are on top of it. Windows 7 Home Premium and above come with lots of backgrounds to choose from. From the same window and during the same personalisation session, you can also apply a screensaver or theme, or perform other similar tasks.

4

Personalise Windows 7 (cont.)

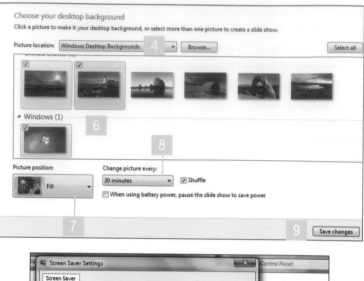

Selecting a new background and screensaver

1. Right-click an empty area of the Desktop.

2. Click Personalize.

3. Click Desktop Background.

4. For Picture location, select Windows Desktop Backgrounds.

5. Use the scroll bars to locate the wallpaper to use as your Desktop background.

6. Select a background to use (or select multiple backgrounds).

7. Select a positioning option (Fill is the best choice).

8. If you have selected multiple backgrounds, choose how often to change the backgrounds.

9. Click Save changes.

After you've selected a new background, click ScreenSaver. If desired, you can also apply a screensaver. A screensaver is a picture or animation that covers your screen and appears after your computer has been idle for a specific amount of time that you set. It used to be that screensavers 'saved' your computer screen from image burn-in, but that is no longer the case. Now, screensavers are used for either visual enhancement or as a security feature. As an extra measure of security, you can configure your screensaver to require a password on waking up, which happens when you move the mouse or hit a key on the keyboard. Requiring a password means that once the screensaver is running, no one but you can log onto your computer, by typing in your password when prompted.

It's important to note that a resource-intensive screensaver – one that has to make a lot of calculations (such as one that offers swimming fish) – can cause problems for netbooks that don't have much RAM or other system resources. The screensaver can hang in a single position, or make it impossible to come out of the screensaver when you move the mouse cursor. If you opt to select a screensaver (or a theme), make sure it's a simple one that doesn't require too much work on the part of your computer.

Changing the screen resolution

1. Click Start.

2. In the Start Search window, type Resolution.

3. Click Adjust screen resolution.

4. Click the arrow next to Resolution and move the slider to the desired position.

5. Click Apply.

6. If prompted to keep these settings, click Yes if you want to, otherwise click Revert.

7. Repeat these steps as desired and select the resolution that is best for you.

Personalise Windows 7 (cont.)

If you're interested, technically, choosing 800 by 600 pixels means that the desktop is shown to you with 800 pixels across and 600 pixels down. A pixel is the smallest unit by which data can be displayed on a computer. So, when you increase the resolution, you increase the number of pixels on the screen. While the science behind resolution is rather complex, suffice it to say that the lower the resolution, the larger your stuff appears on the screen; the higher the resolution, the smaller your stuff appears on the screen.

To sum up this section: you'll want to experiment with your own computer and settings to find the optimal configuration for you. You may want to choose a higher or lower resolution, for instance, keep your Desktop free of unnecessary icons, and create shortcuts on the Desktop for items you use often, such as the My Documents folder or Windows Media Player. You may also want to explore features that make the computer more easily accessible if you have a disability, including applications such as Magnifier, Narrator and On-Screen Keyboard (available from the Ease of Access Center under Accessories).

You're going to have data to save. That data may come in the form of letters you type on the computer, pictures you take using your digital camera, email attachments you want to keep, music you copy from your CD collection, music and media you purchase online, address books, videos from a DV camera, audiobooks you purchase, and more.

Each time you save data, upload pictures, acquire music or download video, you'll be prompted to tell Windows 7 where to save it. To know the answer to that, you need to understand the new Windows 7 libraries. Basically, documents should go in your Documents library, Music in the Music library, Pictures in the Pictures library, and so on. Libraries offer access to two areas: the related personal folder and the public one. (For instance, the Documents library offers access to both the My Documents folder and the Public Documents folder.)

Understand the library structure in Windows 7

4

Personal and public folders

Microsoft understands what types of data you want to save to your computer and built Windows 7's Library structure based on that information. Look at the Start menu. You'll see your name at the top. Clicking your name on the Start menu opens an explorer window, which in turn offers access to your data, downloads, personal data and, yes, libraries, among other things. To see what is shown here, click Libraries in the left pane.

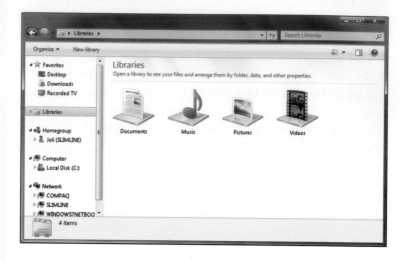

Click the arrow beside Libraries to expand it, then click the arrow under Documents to see two folders there: My Documents and Public Documents. Here's where you'll go to locate data manually. You should keep personal documents in the My Documents folder and documents you want to share in the Public one. (Apply the same rule regarding pictures, music, videos and other data.)

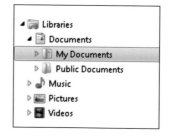

Did you know?

You can also click the Windows Explorer icon on the Taskbar to open an explorer window.

Regarding Public folders: you can share your data and media with Windows 7's built-in Public Folders. There are other ways to share, but Public Folders are extremely easy to use and require no knowledge of permissions, user accounts or network-sharing rules. With Public Folders, you simply move, copy or save the data you want to share in the appropriate Public folder, and anyone with an account on the computer can access it. You can also configure the Public folder to share files with people using other computers on your local network. The nice part is, there's very little configuration involved.

Exploring Windows 7's folder structure

1 Click Start.

2 Click the icon with your name on it.

3 Click the arrow by Libraries. (It won't appear until you hover the mouse over it.)

4 Click the arrow beside Documents.

5 Click My Documents to see the contents of the My Documents folder.

6 Click Public Documents to see the contents of the Public Documents folder.

7 Repeat with Music, Pictures and Videos.

4

See also

Chapter 6 for more on Public folders.

See also

To learn more about sharing, see Chapter 6.

Search folders ▶

Windows 7 lets you search from the Start Search menu, as you know. Just click Start and in the Start Search dialogue box, type a few letters of what you're looking for and results will appear in a list. Here, I've typed Joli and the results are shown.

In these results, there are folders, pictures and contact information, all relating somehow to the word Joli. However, I know there are more results. There are videos, email, documents and more that contain the word Joli or that I've 'tagged' manually to include Joli. In order to locate everything on the computer that has to do with Joli, a more thorough search must be performed. That is easily done by clicking See more results in the results pane.

After clicking See more results, the results will appear in a new window, although they aren't necessarily organised.

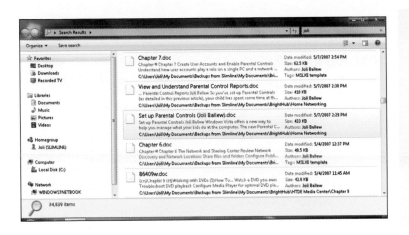

If you're looking for something in particular, you'll probably want to organise the results in a way that promotes actually finding what you want. You can do that by switching the view to Details. Then, you can sort and filter the data by Name, Date modified, Type, Folder and Size by clicking the arrow next to that word in the appropriate column. You switch to Details view using the Views button in the top right corner of the Search window.

Once you perform a search and the results appear in a window, and even after sorting through and filtering the results, you can save the results in a search folder. Once saved, you can access the results any time you like, simply by opening the folder. Search folders are 'smart', too: each time you open the folder after creating it, it performs a new search and adds any new data it finds that matches the search folder's criteria. There are all sorts of uses for search folders, so let your imagination run wild. You can create a search folder for anything you can type into the Start Search dialogue box.

Search folders (cont.)

Did you know?

A search folder only offers a place to access data that matches the search criteria; it does not move the data there or create copies of it.

Creating a search folder

1. Perform a search at the Start menu and click See more results.

2. Click Save search.

3. Name the search appropriately.

4. Click Save.

5. Note the new search folder in the Explorer window, under Favorites.

By default, Windows 7 will turn off the display and put the computer to sleep after a specific amount of idle time. The time that must elapse before this happens depends on the power settings that you've configured for the netbook or laptop, the settings configured by the manufacturer, or the operating system's settings default. It's important to note that when the computer goes to sleep, it uses very little power. Because of this, there's often no need to actually turn off the computer, unless you plan to move it or not use it for a few days, or if you're extremely energy-conscious.

Important !

If you do want to turn off your computer, don't just hit the power button. You need to let Windows 7 handle the shutting-down process. Remember, Windows 7 is an operating system and is there to help you operate your computer system safely and properly.

Shut down Windows 7 safely

Shutting down Windows

1 Click the Start button.

2 Click the arrow by Shut down.

3 Make a choice from what's offered. See page 74 to find out what the options do if you select them.

Did you know? ?

You can also choose to put the computer to sleep or in hibernation, restart the computer, switch users, log off, or lock the computer. Just click the right arrow next to the Shut down button.

4

Shut down Windows 7 safely (cont.)

The options available in the list shown include the following:

- Switch user – if more than one user account is available on the computer, select Switch user to change to another user. Switching users is different from logging off. When you choose to switch users, the current user's program, files, folders and open windows remain intact. When you switch back you do not need to reopen these items. Switching users has nothing to do with putting the computer to sleep or turning it off.

- Log off – choose this option when you want to log off from your computer session. This does not shut down or put the computer to sleep, but will bring up the login in screen. Once logged off, you'll need to log back on, usually by inputting your user name and/or password.

- Lock – use this option to lock the computer. You'll have to input your password to unlock the computer if one is assigned. If a password is not assigned, you'll simply click your user name.

- Restart – use this option to restart the computer. You should restart your computer any time you're prompted to (usually after a Windows 7 update or the installation of a program), when you know an application has stopped working, or the computer seems slow or unresponsive.

- Sleep – use this option to put the computer to sleep. Windows 7's Sleep state uses very little energy and is a better option than turning off the computer completely if you need to use it again soon. Data is stored in RAM and is not lost, and the computer can resume from Sleep quickly.

- Hibernate – similar to Sleep, this puts the computer into hibernation. It also allows you to resume where you left off (like Sleep), but uses less power than Sleep. Coming out of hibernation takes longer than coming out of Sleep, though, so if you're looking for a quick-resume process, choose Sleep.

Join a public or home Wi-Fi network

Introduction

One of the best things about having a netbook or laptop is that it's extremely easy to get online. All come with wireless hardware that enables you to connect to the Internet easily. There are three ways to get online using wireless technology: you can connect to a free Wi-Fi hotspot at a café or similar establishment, connect to an existing home (or business) Wi-Fi network you or someone you trust has set up and configured, and connect using 3G or 4G satellites through a paid subscription to the Internet via an Internet service provider (ISP).

The least expensive way to get online is to get within range of a free Wi-Fi hotspot, which you may find at your local café, pub or library. Free Wi-Fi hotspots offer public access to the Internet, often benefitting the establishment that offers it by enticing customers to purchase a cup of coffee or to have a few drinks at the bar.

Although not free, you will incur no additional costs if you connect to a private Wi-Fi network at your home or your place of work. These networks make it easy to connect and get online without physically connecting with a cable. And because these networks are trustworthy, you don't have to worry (much) about security. You also don't have to go hunting for a free Wi-Fi hotspot!

Finally, if you aren't within range of a free Wi-Fi network and/ or you don't have a Wi-Fi network set up at your house, you won't be able to connect to the Internet unless you've

What you'll do

Locate a hotspot

Enable and disable Wi-Fi

Connect to the Internet using a hotspot

Incorporate the Mobility Center

Troubleshoot with the Network and Sharing Center

Manage the wireless networks list

Consider an always-available internet subscription

purchased a wireless data plan from an ISP. These plans can be expensive, depending on what type you choose. However, with a plan such as this you can access the Internet any time and from anywhere. When you have a subscription service plan, you may not see any reason to seek out and connect to Wi-Fi networks. However, you may find that Wi-Fi hotspots offer faster Internet access than your wireless service provider does, making the idea of hotspots still somewhat enticing. You may also be limited in how much 'bandwidth' you can use each month and want to minimise how much time you spend using your personal wireless connection. Whatever the case, Wi-Fi hotspots are a great way to get online and should be explored.

Wi-Fi hotspots are popping up all over the country. As you know, Wi-Fi hotspots let you connect to the Internet without having to be tethered to an Ethernet cable or tied down with a high monthly wireless bill. Most of the time, at libraries, pubs and cafés anyway, this service is free; however, sometimes it is not. For instance, you may have to buy a cup of coffee, a drink at the bar, or pay for a hotel room, or you may have to give the owner a few pounds to gain access. The first thing you have to do, then, is find one of these hotspots.

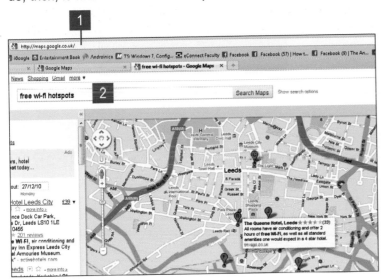

Before you can connect to a Wi-Fi network, the Wi-Fi feature on your netbook or laptop must be enabled. You may have to enable a switch on a laptop or netbook, or use a specific key combination. You should refer to your user's manual to find out exactly how to enable and disable Wi-Fi in this manner. If you can't find a physical switch or button, there are other ways to enable Wi-Fi. One is through the Mobility Center. There's an entire section on the Mobility Center later in this chapter – if necessary, refer to it now to enable Wi-Fi.

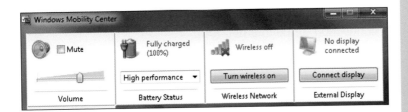

Get online through a hotspot

Locating a hotspot

1 From any computer connected to the Internet, visit *http://maps.google.co.uk*.

2 Type free Wi-Fi hotspots, followed by your city's name.

3 Browse the results.

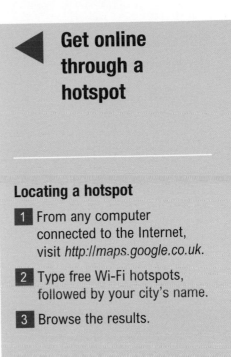

For your information

When wireless is enabled, Windows 7 constantly searches for wireless signals, which uses battery power. That's why people often turn off Wi-Fi when they aren't using it and turn it back on when they want to connect to a Wi-Fi network.

5

Get online through a hotspot (cont.)

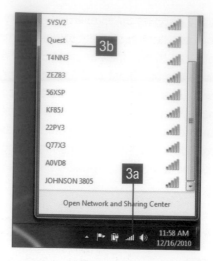

Enabling and disabling Wi-Fi

1 Locate the physical switch or button on the outside of your laptop or netbook that controls Wi-Fi features.

2 Use the switch or button to enable Wi-Fi.

3 To verify Wi-Fi is enabled:

  a. Click the network icon in the Notification area.

  b. Note the available Wi-Fi networks (if there are any).

For your information

If more than one wireless network is available, locate the one that you want to use. Often, this is the one with the most green bars. If you aren't sure, ask someone who is already connected, or is an employee.

Important

Turn off Wi-Fi capabilities any time you are told to do so by an airline pilot. With Wi-Fi turned off you can still use your laptop on a plane, once instructed it's OK to use electronic devices.

When Wi-Fi is enabled, and when you are in range of a Wi-Fi network, you can see the available networks by clicking the Network icon in the Notification area. (You may also see a pop-up, and if you're fast enough, you can click that pop-up to connect.) If you see a network you want to connect to, click it and choose Connect. If it's the first time you've ever connected to this network you may be prompted regarding what type of network it is. Choose Public if you're in a pub, library or café, and choose Work or Home if it's a network you manage, such as one already in your home. Connecting to an existing network allows you to access shared features of the network. In a café that's usually only a connection to the Internet; if it's a home network, it's your personal, shared data (and probably a connection to the Internet, too).

The first image here shows a network in my home; the second shows a public network at my local gym.

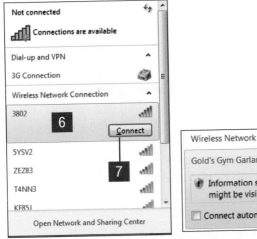

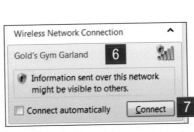

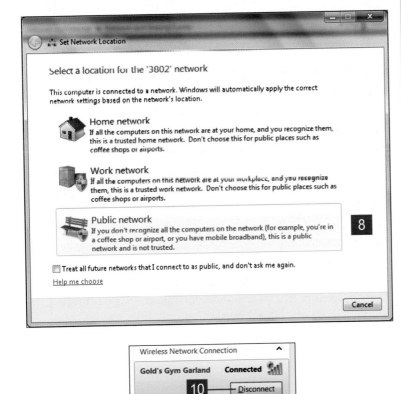

Connecting to the Internet using a hotspot

1 Turn on your wireless computer within range of a wireless network.

2 Enable Wi-Fi.

3 You'll be prompted from the Notification area that wireless networks are available.

4 Click Connect to a network, if you see a pop-up.

5 If you do not see a pop-up (or miss clicking it), click the Network icon in the Notification area of the Taskbar.

6 Click the network to connect to.

7 Click Connect.

8 If prompted to select a network type in the Set Network Location window, choose appropriately.

9 You should be connected automatically, but if you aren't, type the required credentials.

10 Disconnect by clicking the Network icon from the Notification area and selecting Disconnect.

Join a public or home Wi-Fi network 79

Get online through a hotspot (cont.)

For your information

In a public place, if prompted for credentials, ask an employee. If you're at home, use the pass phrase you configured for your network.

Here's a little more information about the Set Network Location options, shown earlier:

- Home – choose this if the network is your home network or a network you trust (such as a network at your parents' house). This connection type lets your computer discover other PCs, printers and devices on the network, and they can see you. It's just for networks you trust!

- Work – choose this if you are connecting to a network at work. The settings for Work and Home are the same as far as we're concerned – only the titles differ so you can tell them apart easily. Choose this for work networks you trust.

- Public – choose this if the network you want to connect to is open to anyone within range, such as networks in cafés, airports and libraries. Windows 7 figures if you choose Public, you want to connect to the Internet and nothing else. It closes down discoverability, so that even your shared data is safe.

One last note about public Wi-Fi hotspots: while you can protect your computer by choosing Public in the Set Network Location dialogue box, you still have to be safe and use common sense while in public. Don't input credit card numbers at a Wi-Fi hotspot (people may see you), don't leave your netbook or laptop unattended, and be aware of your surroundings. Additionally, always disconnect from the network when you've finished using it, just to be on the safe side.

Jargon buster

Discoverability is enabled when you choose the Home or Work network type and allows other computers on the network to see yours and yours to see them. This makes it possible to share data and resources. When you're in a public place, you do not want other computers to be able to discover your computer, so discoverability is disabled.

Windows Mobility Center is available only on laptops and netbooks and offers special features just for users who are on the go. No matter what you own, a laptop or notebook computer, a netbook, a tablet PC, smart PC, or ultra-mobile PC, you've got easy access to power-management options, wireless features, presentation capabilities, battery status and sync options.

Many of these features will prove quite useful, and you'll access them often, including selecting a power plan to improve battery life, using presentation settings when playing a slide show or managing some other type of production, and easily turning off wireless capabilities when on a plane (while still being able to use your computer). All of these options and more are available from the Mobility Center window. So just how does this affect you? Say you're on a plane and the captain announces it's safe to use electronic devices, provided you turn off the wireless feature. You can do that in Mobility Center. While there, you may also want to dim the screen to increase battery life, mute the volume so you don't bother the person sitting beside you, and perhaps sync a mobile device while you have the time.

When you first open the Mobility Center you'll see several squares that contain various features. Here are some of the things you may find in the Mobility Center window (note that some features are dependent on the type of mobile computer you have):

- Brightness – use the slider to adjust the brightness of your display. This will change the brightness only temporarily – it will not change the brightness permanently as it is configured in Control Panel's Power Settings.

- Volume – use the slider to adjust the volume of the speakers or check the Mute box.

- Battery Status – see how much life is left in your battery's current charge. You can also change power plans here.

- Wireless Network – turn your wireless adapter on or off to enable or disable Wi-Fi features.

Mobility Center

5

Mobility Center (cont.)

Incorporating the Mobility Center

1 Click Start.

2 In the Start Search dialogue box, type Mobility.

3 Click Windows Mobility Center under Programs.

■ Screen Rotation – if you are using a tablet PC, you'll have this option. Use it to change the orientation from portrait to landscape, or vice versa.

■ External Display – if you're giving a presentation, such as a PowerPoint birthday or reunion slide show, you can connect an additional monitor to your laptop to show the presentation on. With a secondary monitor, people won't have to crowd around your laptop to see the show.

■ Sync Center – perform Sync Center tasks, such as creating a new partnership, syncing or viewing sync progress.

■ Presentation Settings – adjust what is necessary for giving a presentation. You can turn off the screensaver, change the speaker volume and select a new Desktop background image. You can also access alternate connected displays.

Did you know?

You may see additional settings that are not listed here, supplied by your computer manufacturer. These settings will be specific to your mobile PC and are not part of the mobility settings included with Windows 7.

Programs (1)

Windows Mobility Center   3

Control Panel (1)

Adjust commonly used mobility settings

See more results

Mobility   2   ×

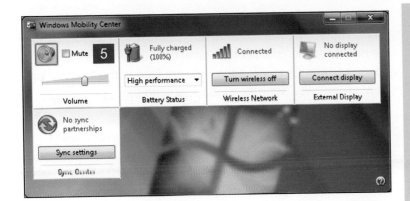

Mobility Center (cont.)

4 Move the slider for Brightness to the left to dim the display; move to the right to brighten it.

5 Check Mute to turn off all sound, or move the slider to the left to lower the sound; move the slider to the right to turn up the sound.

6 Continue exploring as desired.

For your Information

You can increase battery life by turning off wireless connectivity in the Mobility Center, lowering the brightness, and by selecting the Balanced or Power Saver battery plan.

5

Explore the Network and Sharing Center

The Network and Sharing Center contains links and access to everything you'll need to configure, troubleshoot and manage the networks you connect to. You access the Network and Sharing Center by clicking the Network icon in the Notification area, or from the Network window, among other places. The Network and Sharing Center offers lots of features. These are outlined here.

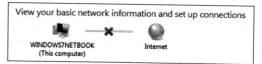

Configuration settings

The main Network and Sharing Center window contains options for viewing network connections and changing default settings. These include:

- Network map – a network map is a graphical representation of the network that shows the relationship between your computer, the local network and the Internet. Red Xs indicate a problem with the network connection. If you don't see any red Xs, the network is functioning properly. If you see a red X, click it. A networking troubleshooter will run and offer suggestions for resolving the problem.

View your basic network information and set up connections

WINDOWS7NETBOOK (This computer)   Internet

- Active networks – this list shows all the connected networks. You can have more than one. For instance, you may have one connection to the Internet and another to a local network.

- Network settings – this list offers options for connecting to a network or troubleshooting one. There's Set up a new connection or network, Connect to a network, Choose homegroup and sharing options (more on this in the next chapter) and Troubleshoot problems.

- Task pane – you can access Control Panel, manage your wireless networks, change adapter settings or change advanced sharing settings.

For our purposes here, we'll focus on troubleshooting connections and managing the list of Wi-Fi networks you've connected to in the past. You'll learn more about how to use the other features of the Network and Sharing Center in the next chapter.

Troubleshoot connections

If there's a problem regarding your connection to a local network, to the Internet, to a Wi-Fi hotspot, to your home network, or a problem with any other network type, you can troubleshoot it in the Network and Sharing Center. For the most part, Wi-Fi-related problems stem from three things:

- You are not within range of the wireless network.

- You have not enabled Wi-Fi capabilities on your computer.

- You have chosen the wrong network location type or have input incorrect credentials.

To troubleshoot any non-working connection, first see whether you can resolve these three most common issues. Move closer to the wireless access point (you can ask where to sit in any public establishment), enable Wi-Fi using the Mobility Center or the button or switch on your computer, or try to reconnect to the network using the Notification area's Network icon options. If you think you've done all of this but are still having problems, open the Network and Sharing Center and click the red X.

5

Explore the Network and Sharing Center (cont.)

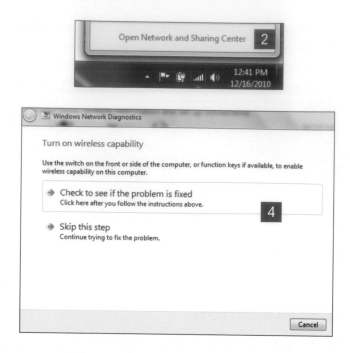

Troubleshooting with the Network and Sharing Center

1 Click the Network icon in the Notification area.

2 Click Open Network and Sharing Center.

3 Click the red X that denotes a non-working connection.

4 Perform the solutions offered.

If you find that the only option is to plug in an Ethernet cable to access the network (or you are informed that no wireless network adapter can be found), there may be a problem with the wireless adapter inside your computer. You probably can't do anything about that without the help of a professional. However, you can check Device Manager, available in Windows 7, to see whether it recognises a problem. If there is a problem, you can try to install a new driver, start the wireless adapter, or perform other tasks.

Every wireless network you've ever connected to is listed in the Manage wireless networks list. This helps Windows 7 remember networks you've connected to, so that you don't have to input credentials each time or manually connect. When Windows 7 looks for a network, it starts at the top of this list and works its way down. If you've connected to a lot of Wi-Fi networks, this list could be getting pretty long. The longer the list, the longer it can take to locate the network you want and connect to it. This is especially true if the network you use the most is at the bottom of the list. You should occasionally check this list and make sure that you still use the networks listed there. You should also rearrange the list and put your most accessed networks at the top.

Did you know?

You can easily rename a network by right-clicking it in the Manage wireless networks list.

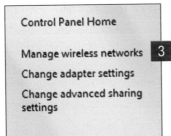

Control Panel Home

Manage wireless networks   3

Change adapter settings

Change advanced sharing settings

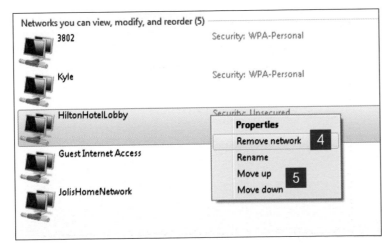

Networks you can view, modify, and reorder (5)

3802   Security: WPA-Personal

Kyle   Security: WPA-Personal

HiltonHotelLobby   Security: Unsecured

Guest Internet Access

JolisHomeNetwork

Properties
Remove network   4
Rename
Move up   5
Move down

Manage wireless networks

Managing the wireless networks list

1 Click the network icon in the Notification area.

2 Click Open Network and Sharing Center.

3 Click Manage wireless networks.

4 Right-click any connection to remove the connection from the list. Click Remove network.

5 Right-click any network to move up or down and select Move up or Move down, as applicable. Move the networks you use often to the top of the list.

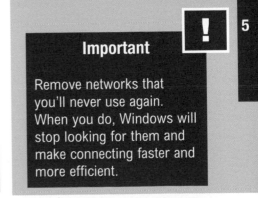

Important

Remove networks that you'll never use again. When you do, Windows will stop looking for them and make connecting faster and more efficient.

5

Consider always-available Internet ▶

If you aren't within range of a Wi-Fi network very often, either at home or on the road, and you really need more reliable access to the Internet, consider an always-available Internet subscription. Providers which offer this service have varying rate plans, some of which offer unlimited access. Others may offer plans that keep track of how much data you send and receive and charge you accordingly. This more limited type of plan is generally OK, provided you can combine it with Wi-Fi access fairly often. You won't be able to use a limited-data plan if you have no other way to access the Internet; you'd run out of service time before the month was up, for sure!

It'll be up to you to research the plans available to you. If you have an existing service with a provider that offers you mobile phone service, cable TV or digital phone, you may be able to get an add-on plan for your laptop or netbook at a cheaper price than if you went with another company. You may also be able to get service from the store that sold you the netbook or laptop. Of course, you can always ask your friends what they use. The point is, do your homework. Once you get locked into one of these plans, you could be stuck with it for a while!

Connect and share with a home network

Introduction

If you have more than one computer in your home or if you have an Internet connection you pay for, you should set up a *network* so that you can share that connection as well as media, data, calendars and hardware such as printers and media extenders. Network hardware can allow connections through an Ethernet cable or through Wi-Fi, or both, depending on the hardware that you purchased when you set up the network. (You can also configure a direct connection with a specialised cable or use Bluetooth to connect to a single computer, among other, rarer options.)

Connecting with Wi-Fi enables you to access the Internet and the home network using your laptop or netbook from anywhere in the house or its surrounding areas, such as the garden or garage. You learned about this type of connection in Chapter 5 and how to connect with it. Connecting with an Ethernet cable enables you to access the Internet and home network, too, but because this requires you to connect physically to the network hardware, you can't roam around unhindered. You may have to connect this way when at a friend's house, or if your network hardware (router, switch or hub) supports Ethernet connections only and does not offer Wi-Fi. For the most part, though, Ethernet is faster than Wi-Fi, so you may opt to connect using this method while at your desk or close to the network access point anyway. You'll get a faster connection connecting in this manner – Ethernet's not all bad.

What you'll do

Connect with Ethernet

Verify network discovery is enabled

Configure sharing

Move files to a public folder

Share a personal folder

Create a subfolder

Create a library

Copy or move a file

Move and copy with Cut, Copy and Paste

Create or join a homegroup

Find out what you can access on the network

It doesn't matter how you connect, through a wireless connection or a wired one: connecting isn't all of it, especially when it comes to home networks. Once connected, you'll need to know how to get the most from your network. This means configuring sharing properly, placing data in the appropriate folders, utilising the Public folders, managing the data you want to share and keep, diagnosing connectivity problems and, finally, creating a homegroup, if applicable.

For your information

If you need to create a network, you'll have to purchase and install the required network hardware (preferably a wired/wireless hybrid router) and then use the Network and Sharing Center in Windows 7 to set it up and configure it. Once you've done that you can connect to it from your laptop or netbook.

Most of the time, you'll connect to wireless networks with your netbook or laptop. Occasionally, however, perhaps when you are at home, a friend's or a relative's, or staying in a hotel that offers only wired access to the Internet, you'll have to connect physically. You will do this using an Ethernet cable. You may also want to connect using Ethernet while at your desk near the router if you want a faster connection than with Wi-Fi. You probably have only one Ethernet port on the outside of your computer. The cable will snap into this port and snap into the network device, probably a router.

Connecting with Ethernet

1 Turn on your netbook or laptop and log in if necessary.

2 Connect the Ethernet cable to the Ethernet port on the netbook or laptop. It should snap into place.

3 Connect the other end of the Ethernet cable to an available port on the router, switch or hub. It should snap into place.

4 Wait one minute while the network initialises the connection.

5 Choose Home if at home, Work if at work. Choose Public only if you're in a hotel or some other public establishment.

6 If your network is protected with a pass phrase, type it in. You need to do this only the first time you connect.

! Important

You must choose Home to access all the desired features in a home network, including media streaming and sharing, among other things.

Connect with Ethernet (cont.)

If you connected physically to your home network using an Ethernet cable (or tried to connect using Wi-Fi) but couldn't see the network, there are a few things to verify. First, your home network needs to be configured as Home or Work and you should have opted to share data on it (which you can check in a later section of this chapter). Second, you need to make sure that on your laptop or netbook, the one you're trying to connect with, network discovery is enabled.

Verifying network discovery is enabled

1 Click the network icon in the Taskbar's Notification area.

2 Click Open Network and Sharing Center.

3 In the left pane of the Network and Sharing Center, click Change advanced sharing settings.

4 Under Home or Work (current profile), click Turn on network discovery.

5 Click Save changes.

6 Repeat the steps in the previous section to join the network.

Important

If you plan to share media on your network, choose Home.

Change sharing options for different network profiles

Windows creates a separate network profile for each network you use. You can choose specific options for each profile.

Home or Work (current profile)

Network discovery

When network discovery is on, this computer can see other network computers and devices and is visible to other network computers. What is network discovery?

4 — ● Turn on network discovery
○ Turn off network discovery

In order to create an effective home network, you need to share data and printers, among other things. The Network and Sharing Center offers the option Change advanced sharing settings in the Task pane to help you here. Click it to access the sharing options you'll want to configure or verify are configured effectively. Here are a few things you'll see and a few things to check:

■ Network discovery – this section lets you configure options related to network discovery. These settings are configured automatically based on the network type you chose when you connected (Home, Work, Public). However, you can override those settings here and configure additional settings. Network discovery should be enabled on your laptop and your other networked computers.

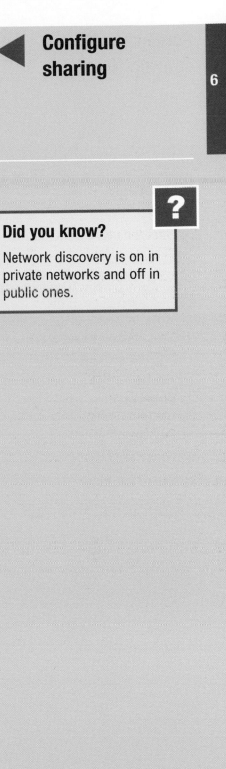

Change sharing options for different network profiles

Windows creates a separate network profile for each network you use. You can choose specific options for each profile.

Home or Work (current profile) ⌃

Network discovery

When network discovery is on, this computer can see other network computers and devices and is visible to other network computers. What is network discovery?

◉ Turn on network discovery
◯ Turn off network discovery

File and printer sharing

When file and printer sharing is on, files and printers that you have shared from this computer can be accessed by people on the network.

◉ Turn on file and printer sharing
◯ Turn off file and printer sharing

■ File and printer sharing – this section offers settings for the shared data you've set up yourself and printers you've installed and shared. File and printer sharing is on in private networks and off in public ones. On a home network, enable file and printer sharing.

■ Public folder sharing – this section offers a way to turn public folder sharing on or off. If you turn on Public folder sharing, any data you put in shared folders will be available to network users as well as others who access your computer as guests or users with their own computer account. We think it's best to enable Public folder sharing and put data in the Public folders that you want to share with others on your home network.

Configure sharing

Did you know?

Network discovery is on in private networks and off in public ones.

Configure sharing (cont.)

Configuring sharing

1 Click the network icon in the Taskbar's Notification area.

2 Click Open Network and Sharing Center.

3 In the left pane of the Network and Sharing Center, click Change advanced sharing settings.

4 Configure sharing options as desired.

5 If applicable, click Save changes.

- Media sharing – this section allows you to enable media sharing so that others on the network can access shared media. We suggest enabling this if you want to access and share media on your home network.

- Password protected sharing – this section allows you to enable sharing but requires a password for access. Users who have access to the network are required to input a valid user name and password before accessing shared resources.

- Windows homegroup connections – homegroup computers are computers and devices that are part of the homegroup you create. Typically, Windows manages this. However, you can manually manage homegroup settings by selecting Use user accounts and passwords to connect to other computers. We don't suggest changing this.

?

Did you know?

A homegroup lets you easily share music, pictures, videos and documents among home computers that run Windows 7 or any compatible media devices. You can create a homegroup as soon as you set up your network if you choose Home network in the Set network location window.

The main reason people create a network is to share data, printers, media and an Internet connection. In this section, we'll talk about sharing data. There are two ways to share data: you can either put the data you want to share in the built-in Public folders, or you can share data using personal folders you create or manage. You can use a combination of the two as well. How do you know which to use and when? Here are some things to take into consideration.

Public folder sharing

Public folders are already built into the Windows 7 folder structure. The Public folder contains several subfolders, including Public Downloads, Public Documents, Public Music, Public Pictures, Public Videos and Recorded TV. You can create your own folders here, too. To share data using the folders, simply save or place the data there. Then, anyone who has access to the computer or network can easily look at what's in the folders.

Use the Public folder for sharing if:

- you want every person with a user account on the computer to be able to access what's in the folder

- you want to share files and folders from a single location on your computer

Connect and share with a home network 95

Utilise the Public folders (cont.)

Moving files to a Public folder

1 Locate data you'd like to move to a Public folder.

2 Select the data. Note you can select multiple files by holding down the Ctrl key while selecting, and you can select entire folders.

3 Right-click the selected data and click Cut.

4 Locate the desired Public folder.

5 Right-click inside the folder and click Paste.

- you want to be able to quickly access, view and modify everything you have shared

- you want everything you are sharing kept separate from the data you do not want to share

- you do not need to configure different sharing rules for different people who have access – you are OK with everyone having access to the data you put there and everyone being able to do what they wish with the data

- you prefer to use the default shared settings and do not want to manually share data or configure any advanced settings

You can locate the Public folders by clicking the folder icon on the Taskbar. Then position your mouse over any library and click the triangle. You can then see the two libraries for that specific library. In the image here, Public Pictures is selected and is available from the Pictures library.

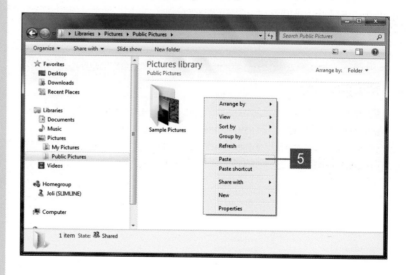

Did you know?

You can create a shortcut to any folder, even a Public one, on the Desktop. Just locate the folder, right-click it and choose Send To, Desktop (create shortcut).

Your personal folders and any folders you create yourself can be shared. In contrast to using Public folders for sharing, with personal folder sharing you have much more control over the shared data.

Use any folder for sharing if:

- you want to share data directly from your personal folders, such as Documents, Pictures or Music, and do not want to have to re-save or move data you want to share to your Public folder

- you want to allow some users the ability to change the data in the shared folders while at the same time only allowing others to view it. Additionally, you want to completely block others from accessing the data at all (you can't do this with Public folder sharing)

- you share large files that would be burdensome to copy and manage in a separate shared folder.

?

Did you know?

When you share a folder, you can configure who can access the folder by right-clicking it. Click Share with to see your options. After selecting an option, you can configure other sharing details, if applicable.

Sharing a personal folder

1 Locate a folder to share. In this example, I'll share the My Documents folder.

2 Right-click the folder.

3 Click Share with.

4 Select homegroup (Read), homegroup (Read/Write), nobody or specific people.

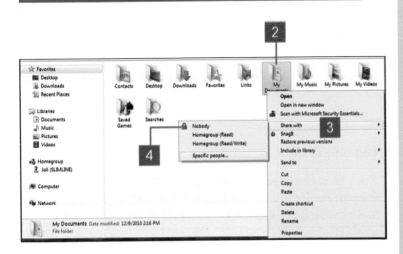

Personal folder sharing (cont.)

5 If you opt to share with specific people:

a. Type the name of the person in the Add area.

b. Click Add.

c. Click the arrow by Read and select the appropriate option.

d. Click Share.

e. Click Done.

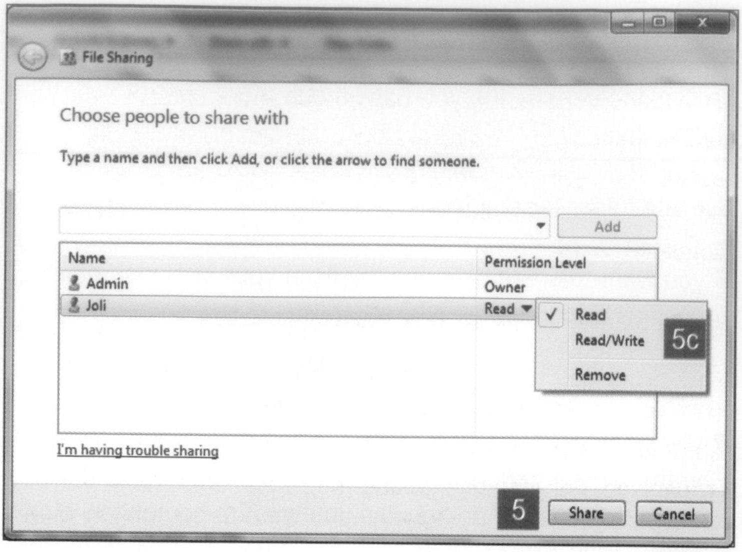

File Sharing

Choose people to share with

Type a name and then click Add, or click the arrow to find someone.

	Add

Name	Permission Level
Admin	Owner
Joli	Read ▼

✓ Read
Read/Write **5c**
Remove

I'm having trouble sharing

5 Share   Cancel

Jargon buster

Read – users can view the data but cannot make changes to it.

Read/Write – users can view and change the shared data.

To manage the data you keep and share with users on your network, you need to know how to do a few things. First, you'll want to know how to create a library to organise specific data. You can share data in the library if you like. Beyond that, you need to know how to create subfolders, and copy, move and delete files and folders or keep them organised, among other things.

Create subfolders and new libraries

While Windows 7's default folders and libraries will suit your needs for a while, it won't last. Soon you'll need to create subfolders inside those folders to manage your data and keep it organised. For instance, inside the Documents folder you may need to create a subfolder called Tax Information to hold scanned receipts, tax records and account information. Inside the Pictures folder you might create folders named 2009, 2010, 2011, or Weddings, Holidays, Pets, and so on.

Did you know?

You can create a folder just about anywhere: on the desktop, in an existing folder, or in a folder you create yourself. If you have an external hard drive or networked computer, you can create a folder called Backup in any of the Public folders and store backup data there if you like.

Creating subfolders in the existing folders often works just fine. Sometimes, though, you may have specific hobbies or interests that require you to create your own library. In this case, you'd extend what's in the left pane of your library by adding your own link under Libraries to the mix. Here, I've created a new library called Pets, and its associated icon appears in the main window of my Libraries folder.

Work with files and folders

6

Creating a subfolder

1 Open any folder or established library.

2 Click New folder.

3 Name the folder.

4 Press Enter on the keyboard.

Did you know?

A library offers access to data you have stored elsewhere on your computer; the data is not actually moved into the library. For instance, a Pets library may offer access to pictures in the Public Pictures folder, veterinary records from the My Documents folder, and information about a non-profit organisation you donate to located in a folder you created yourself.

Work with files and folders (cont.)

Creating a library

1 Click Start.

2 Click your personal folder – that's the one with your name on it.

3 Right-click Libraries.

4 Click New, then click Library.

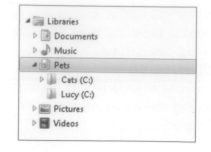

The idea behind extending Windows 7's library and/or folder structure is to personalise it to meet your needs. If you travel a lot, you may want to create an entirely new library called Travel and configure access to folders and subfolders you've created and named for the cities or countries you've visited, travel documents, and even videos. Alternatively, you could create a Travel folder in the My Pictures folder to hold pictures you've taken, a Travel folder in the My Documents folder to hold travel information, and a third Travel folder in the My Videos folder to hold videos you've amassed.

The window that opens when you click your name from the Start menu offers access to Windows 7's default libraries such as Documents and Pictures as well as your default folders such as My Documents and My Pictures. When you're ready to create additional libraries, folders and subfolders, this is the place to create them.

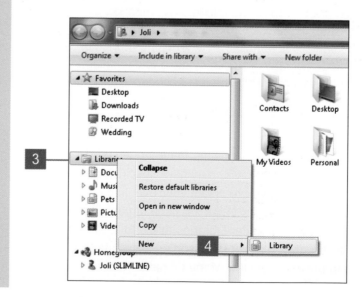

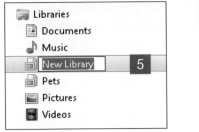

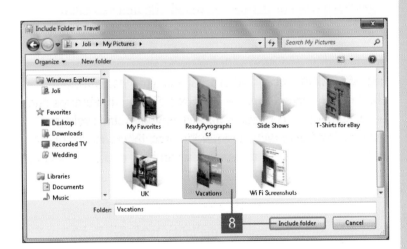

5 Type a name for the new library. (If the library name is not highlighted like this, right-click once and click Rename.)

6 Click Enter (or Return) on the keyboard.

7 The new folder will appear alphabetically in the list, by default.

8 Click the new folder and click Include folder.

9 Locate a folder to add and click Include folder.

10 To add another folder, in the new library, click what now says 1 location. You can add locations there.

Copy, move and delete files ▶

After folders and subfolders, the next logical step is to put data in those folders. This will help you keep the data organised and easily available. Before you start moving data around, though, it's important to understand the difference between copying and moving. When you copy something, an exact duplicate is made. The original copy of the data remains where it is and a copy is placed somewhere else. For the most part, this is not what you want to do when organising data. Rather, you want to move the data into the appropriate folders (you don't want duplicates).

When you back up data you want to copy it. And you'll want to copy the data to a source you'll keep away from your laptop or netbook. We can't stress how important it is to back up data on a laptop, because it can be so easily lost, damaged or stolen. You can copy data to a CD or DVD drive, external hard drive, flash drive or network drive, among other places.

To move and copy data, you have quite a few choices. The first is to drag and drop with the trackball or a mouse. You can left-click and drag and drop the data, or you can right-click and drag and drop the data. Left-clicking may be easier (especially if you connect an external mouse), but there are rules to remember. When you right-click, there are no rules to remember. When you right-click and drag and drop, you have the option to move or to copy when you drop the data. When you left-click and drag and drop, certain things happen by default when you drop the data. If you drag and drop data from a folder to the desktop, the folder is always moved. If you drag and drop from one folder to another, again, the file is moved out of the original folder and into the new one. If you drag and drop from one folder on one hard drive to a folder on another, the data is copied. Windows 7 assumes in this case that you are backing up data to a secondary source and don't want to move it. There are more rules, but let's cut our losses. *If you right-click and drag and drop data, you get to choose what to do with the data.* You can copy, move, create a shortcut, or even cancel.

For your information

The highlighted note may say 'move' when dragging a file, but you'll get a choice when you drop it.

Deleting files and folders is as simple as right-clicking and selecting Delete. When you delete an item, library or folder the deleted data goes to the Recycle Bin. If you delete something by mistake, you can get it back if need be, by opening the Recycle Bin, locating the data and clicking Restore. Note that once you empty the Recycle Bin, that data is no longer available for restoring.

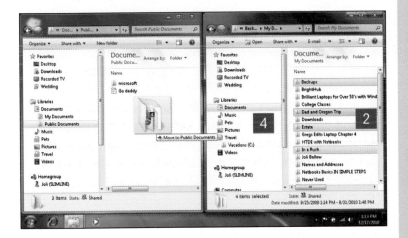

You can also move and copy data using the commands Cut, Copy and Paste. You access these commands from the window's Organize menu or by right-clicking.

- Cut – copies the data to Windows 7's clipboard (a virtual, temporary holding area). The data will be deleted from its original location as soon as you 'paste' it somewhere else. Pasting cut data moves the data.

- Copy – copies the data to Windows 7's clipboard. The data will *not* be deleted from its original location even when you 'paste' it somewhere else. Pasting copied data will copy the data, not move it.

Copying or moving a file (or files, a folder, or multiple folders)

1 Locate data to move or copy.

2 Select the data. (Hold down the Ctrl key to select non-contiguous data; use the Shift key to select contiguous data.)

3 Hold down the right trackball button and drag, or use the right button on an attached mouse.

4 Drop the data into the appropriate folder or subfolder.

5 Choose Move Here or Copy Here.

Delete a file (or files, folder, or folders)

1 Right-click any file or folder you want to delete.

2 Click Delete.

Copy, move and delete files (cont.)

Moving and copying with Cut, Copy and Paste

1 Right-click any data you want to move or copy.

2 To move the data, click Cut. To copy the data, click Copy.

3 Browse to the location to copy or move the file.

4 Right-click and select Paste.

■ Paste – copies or moves the data to the new location. If the data was cut, it will be moved; if the data was copied, it will be copied.

A homegroup is a new feature in Windows 7 that allows you to simplify the task of sharing media, documents, printers and data on your home network. You may have created a homegroup during the network set-up process, or when you set up your Windows 7 computer when you initialised it. However, if you did not create a homegroup then, or if you have an existing homegroup on your network and want to join it, you can do so from the Network and Sharing Center.

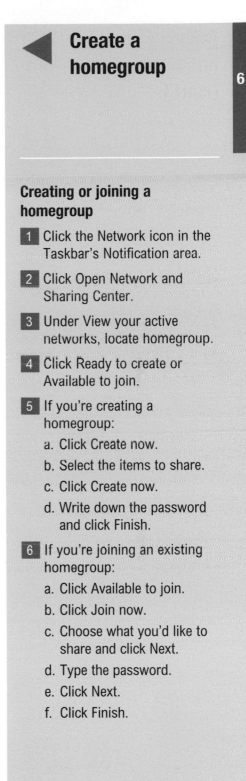

Create a homegroup

6

Creating or joining a homegroup

1 Click the Network icon in the Taskbar's Notification area.

2 Click Open Network and Sharing Center.

3 Under View your active networks, locate homegroup.

4 Click Ready to create or Available to join.

5 If you're creating a homegroup:

  a. Click Create now.

  b. Select the items to share.

  c. Click Create now.

  d. Write down the password and click Finish.

6 If you're joining an existing homegroup:

  a. Click Available to join.

  b. Click Join now.

  c. Choose what you'd like to share and click Next.

  d. Type the password.

  e. Click Next.

  f. Click Finish.

Create a homegroup (cont.)

Did you know?

You can view the homegroup password from Control Panel, Network and Internet, homegroup if you forget it. You can also change the password there. If you're joining an existing homegroup, you'll have to get the password from another homegroup computer.

If you've connected to your home network you should be able to access several things, provided the network 'administrator' has configured sharing on the network. You should be able to access the data in the Public folders, shared printers and other hardware, and whatever personal data has been personally and specifically shared by users on the network. Of course, what you can and cannot access depends on how sharing is set up. It may be locked down pretty tight, requiring you to input a user name and password to gain access, or it may have file and printer sharing or even Public folder sharing disabled.

You should be able to access the Internet from just about any local area Ethernet network you can connect to, even if you can't access the local resources on it. If you're in a hotel, for instance, you can access the Internet, but you probably can't access the computer at the front desk or the file server in the basement. However, you may be able to access a shared printer (if you're a registered guest) for printing boarding passes and receipts. The network administrator decides who can access what on a local network, and only those with the proper credentials (user name and password) can access protected files and hardware. The best way to see what access you have is to try to access the resources on the network. Although there are several ways to do this, using Windows Explorer is often the most straightforward.

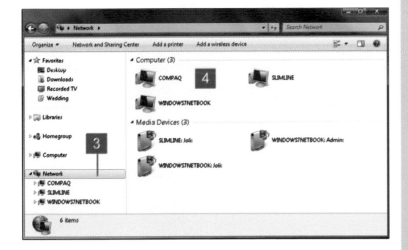

Finding out what you can access on the network

1. Click the folder icon on the Taskbar.

2. Locate the homegroup icon in the left pane. Click it to see homegroup computers. (You may not have a homegroup.)

3. Click Network in the left pane.

4. Notice the computers and resources on your network. Double-click any computer icon.

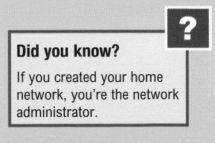

Did you know?

If you created your home network, you're the network administrator.

Find out what you can access on the network (cont.)

Important

If you can't access a network computer, go to that computer and create a user name and apply a password for yourself. You should be able to get access then.

5 If prompted, input user credentials and a password. You can try the user name and password you use on your laptop or netbook, but if that doesn't work, you'll have to input a user name and password for a user on the computer you're trying to access.

6 If you wish, tick Remember my credentials and then click OK.

7 Once you have access, take a look at the shared resources. Here you can see:

   a. Two shared printers.

   b. A shared CD/DVD drive (e).

   c. A Themes folder.

   d. A Users folder.

Important

The first time you connect from your laptop or netbook to a shared printer, either to view the print queue or to print a document or picture, a driver will be installed for that printer onto your computer.

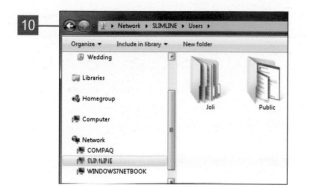

10

Find out what you can access on the network (cont.)

8 Double-click the Users folder.

9 You may have access only to the Public folder, or you may have access to the user's personal folders, too.

10 Click the Back button and continue experimenting as desired.

Surf the Internet

Introduction

Windows 7 comes with Internet Explorer (IE) 8, an application you can use to surf the Internet. Internet Explorer 8 is a 'web browser' and it has everything you need. It has a pop-up blocker, tools you can use to save your favourite web pages so you can access them easily later, the ability set multiple home pages that open when IE does, an easy way to sign up for and read RSS feeds, and even a few things you've probably never tried before, including accelerators, web slices and InPrivate Browsing.

You may be aware of other web browsers and want to use one of them on your laptop or netbook. In fact, you may use Firefox, Safari, Chrome or another browser on your desktop PC. If you prefer any of these browsers, you can certainly use them on your laptop or netbook; we can't see any reason why you shouldn't (except that IE has a lot of really cool features you'll miss out on). However, if you're thinking one browser is noticeably faster than another, that's probably not true, nor is it a good reason to move away from IE. In fact, almost every web browser will claim it's the fastest and most secure. While some of these claims may be relatively true (for instance, Safari may actually be 'safer' than IE because more hackers will go after IE than Safari), for the most part, the speed at which you surf the Web has more to do with your Internet connection and the number of add-ons you have attached to your browser. Likewise, security has a lot to do with common sense and anti-virus/malware/spyware software.

If you're not sure which browser to use or whether you should switch, give IE a try. It's already installed, it's safe and secure, and it's what we'll discuss in this chapter!

What you'll do

Explore tabbed browsing

Set a home page

Mark a Favorite

Organise your Favorites list

Use accelerators

Use web slices

Subscribe to RSS feeds

Work with RSS feeds

View and clear History

Use InPrivate Browsing

Disable unnecessary add-ons

Explore the interface

You can open IE8 in a number of ways. On the Taskbar, look for the big blue E. Click it once to open the program. You can also open Internet Explorer from the Start menu, from the All Programs list – it's near the top. You may even find an icon for IE on the Desktop.

There are several parts to the Internet Explorer interface. These include but are not limited to:

- Address bar – used to type in Internet addresses, also known as URLs (uniform resource locators). Generally, an Internet address takes the form of *www.companyname.com*.

- Command bar – used to access icons such as the Home and Print icons. See Table 7.1 for a list of icons and their uses.

- Tabs – used to access and switch between websites when multiple sites are open.

- Search window – used to search for anything on the Internet.

- Status bar – used to find information about the current activity.

- Favorites tab – used to access your list of saved websites, called Favorites.

Did you know?

Because IE8 uses new technologies for obtaining web data, if you come across a website that does not look or 'act' the way you think it should, you can click Compatibility View Settings under the Tools menu.

Table 7.1 Command bar icons from left to right

Command bar icon	What it does
Favorites Center	View Favorites you've added, RSS feeds and browsing history. (You may also see the Favorites bar, which contains quick links to your favourite Favorites!)
Tabs	Access open tabs
Home	Access your home page (or home pages). This icon includes a drop-down menu, too, which lets you change your home page(s) and add and remove home page(s)
Add web slices/RSS feeds	Click to get access to content on the current web page
Read mail	Access to Windows Live Mail if it is installed
Print	Print a web page (or part of one)
Page	Offers a drop-down menu that allows access to all accelerators, as well as special features such as Blog with Windows Live and Translate with Bing
Safety	Offers a drop-down list that lets you delete your browsing history, view security reports, read a website's privacy policy, and more
Tools	Offers a drop-down menu that lets you access security feature configuration, Internet options and personalisation options
Help	Offers a drop-down menu to access Help pages, get online support and learn more about Internet Explorer
Blog This	Allows you to blog about the current page using Windows Live Writer, if it is installed

7

Jargon buster

Blog means to write something to a web page, such as Windows Live Spaces. Blog comes from two words, web and log. Most blogs are opinion pieces.

Explore the interface (cont.)

There are a few words you're going to see often, including URL, link, website, among others. To get the most out of this chapter, you need to know what these mean. Here are some terms you should know before continuing:

- Domain name – for our use here, a domain name is synonymous with a website name.

- Favorite – a web page for which you've chosen to maintain a shortcut in the Favorites Center.

- Home page – the web page that opens when you open IE8. You can set the home page and configure additional pages to open as well.

- Link – a shortcut to a web page. Links are often offered in an email, document or web page to allow you to access a site without having to actually type in its name. In almost all instances, links are underlined and in a different colour than the page they are configured on.

- Load – a web page must 'load' before you can access it. Some pages load instantly while others take a few seconds.

- Navigate – the process of moving from one web page to another or viewing items on a single web page. Often the term is used as follows: 'Click the link to navigate to the new web page.'

- Search – a term used when you type a word or group of words into a Search window. Searching for data produces results.

- Scroll Up and Scroll Down – a process of using the scroll bars on a web page or the arrow keys on a keyboard to move up and down the pages of a website.

- Website – a group of web pages that contains related information. Microsoft's website contains information about Microsoft products, for instance.

- URL – the information you type to access a website, for example *www.microsoft.com*.

A long time ago in a land far, far away, if you wanted to have more than one web page open, you had to open another instance of IE. Now it's easy to have multiple web pages open with the addition of 'tabs'. Here, four tabs are open for four different web pages: one for Google, one for Facebook, one for Yahoo! and another to log into a web-based email account. After the Log In tab you can make out a blank tab. To open a fifth tab, you click this empty tab and browse to the site you would like to visit.

Exploring tabbed browsing

1 With Internet Explorer open, in the Address bar type *www.microsoft.com/uk*.

2 Look for a link named Support. Hover the mouse over it to see the options.

3 Right-click Windows 7.

7

Did you know?

If you can't see the Menu bar – the one with File, Edit, View, etc. – click the Alt key once on your keyboard.

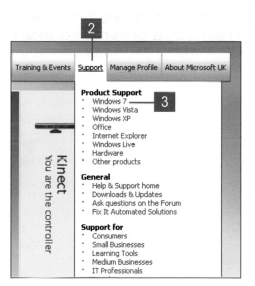

Explore tabbed browsing (cont.)

4 Click Open in New Tab.

5 Click the new tab to see the web page content.

6 Click the blank tab at the end of the tab group.

7 Note the options, including to browse with an InPrivate session, detailed later.

Timesaver tip

Click Ctrl + T to open a new tab using the keyboard.

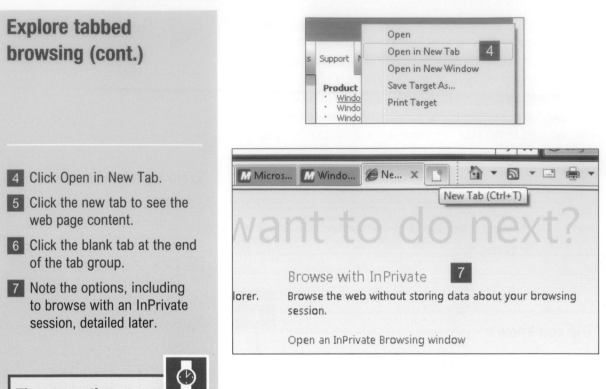

You may recall that the earliest versions of Internet Explorer let you mark a web page as your home page and this page would be displayed each time you opened the program. Starting with Internet Explorer 7, you can now assign multiple web pages as home pages. With multiple pages marked, when you start IE8, each website automatically loads in its own tab.

There are a number of ways to assign web pages as home pages, but you should always navigate to the pages first. Once you've opened a web page you want to add as a home page, click the arrow next to the Home button and choose Add or Change Home Page. You can then choose from three options:

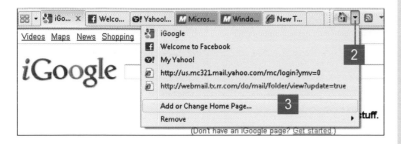

- Use this webpage as your only home page – select this option if you want only one page to serve as your home page.

- Add this webpage to your home page tabs – select this option if you want this page to be one of several home pages.

- Use the current tab set as your home page – select this option if you've opened multiple tabs and you want all of them to be home pages.

◀ **Set a home page**

7

Setting a home page

1 In IE8, use the Address bar to locate a web page you want to use as your home page.

2 Click the arrow next to the Home icon.

3 Click Add or Change Home Page.

4 Make a selection using the information provided regarding each option.

5 Click Yes.

6 Repeat these steps as necessary.

Timesaver tip

Save four or five web pages as your home page group. It will make accessing your favourite pages quicker and you won't have to struggle to find them.

Mark a Favorite ▶

Favorites are websites you save links to for accessing more easily at a later time. They differ from home pages because by default they do not open when you start IE8. The Favorites you save appear in the Favorites Center, which you can access by clicking the yellow star on the Command bar. You may see some Favorites listed already, including Microsoft Websites and MSN Websites. Every time you save a Favorite, it will appear here. It's also possible, as you can see here, to create your own folders to organise the Favorites you keep.

? Did you know?

You can also access Favorites from the Favorites menu (which you can access by pressing Alt on the keyboard).

 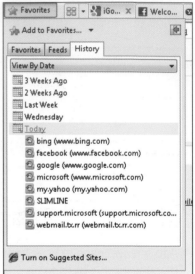

In addition to holding links to your favourite websites, the Favorites Center includes access to History and Feeds. Feeds contain links to RSS feeds to which you've subscribed (detailed later in this chapter). History lists the links to the web pages you visited recently. Take a look at the History list here.

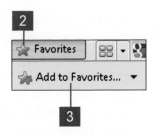

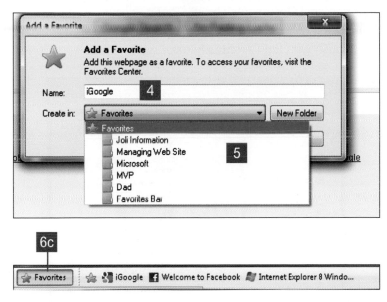

Marking a Favorite

1. Navigate to a web page to add as a Favorite.

2. Click the Favorites icon.

3. Click Add to Favorites.

4. Name the Favorite.

5. Choose where to create the Favorite. Note you can:

   a. Save it to the Favorites list.

   b. Save it to a folder you've already created.

   c. Create a new folder.

6. To view other options for adding a Favorite:

   a. Repeat steps 1 and 2.

   b. Click the arrow beside Add to Favorites.

   c. Make the appropriate choice. Note you can save a Favorite to the Favorites bar, shown here.

7

Did you know?

The Favorites bar is a new toolbar that appears above the tabs in IE. You can save Favorites there. If you use a netbook, though, you may want to save that space so that you can see more of the web page.

?

Mark a Favorite (cont.)

Organising your Favorites list

1 Click Start.

2 Click your user name.

3 Double-click the Favorites folder to open it.

4 To create a new folder, click New Folder. Name the folder appropriately.

5 Drag and drop Favorites into the subfolders you've created.

6 Continue organising as desired.

There will probably come a time when your Favorites Center becomes unwieldy. Perhaps you haphazardly saved Favorites and now need to organise them, or maybe you have Favorites you want to delete. You may even have Favorites you want to move to another folder. You can do this inside the Favorites Center by dragging and dropping files between folders. However, a better way is to open the Favorites folder inside your personal Documents library. That's because each time you make a change in the Favorites Center, it closes. This does not happen with the Favorites folder.

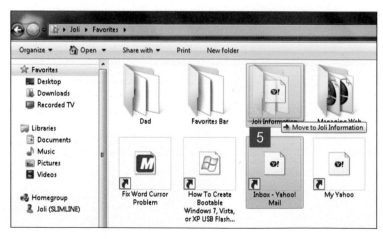

? Did you know?

You can delete an entire folder or a single Favorite link by right-clicking and choosing Delete.

One of the most common tasks you'll do in IE8 is to copy data from a web page. You'll copy an address and then paste that address into a mapping website to obtain a route. You'll copy a map and then paste it into an email to send to someone else. You may even copy data from one website and then go to another to find its meaning or to translate what you've copied into another language. All of these tasks take several clicks and quite a bit of work. Accelerators let you perform these most common copy and paste tasks more quickly.

There are many accelerators, and web designers can create their own. Some of the more common accelerators you may see include:

- Blog with Windows Live
- Email with Windows Live
- Map with Bing
- Search with Bing
- Translate with Bing.

To access an accelerator, highlight any data on a web page and then click the accelerator icon. This icon is a blue arrow. (Alternatively, you can right-click.)

Use accelerators

Using accelerators

1 Open any web page in IE8.

2 Copy any data on the page. For the purpose of this exercise, if possible, select an address.

3 Locate the accelerator icon and click it.

4 Click any option. Here, I've selected Map with Bing. Note the map.

5 If desired, click the map for additional directions.

7

Use accelerators (cont.)

Beyond mapping an address, though, if you incorporate Windows Live Essentials programs as outlined in Chapter 8, you can easily use Windows Live to blog about a specific item you've selected, email something you've selected, and more. It's just another reason to consider grouping Windows 7 with Internet Explorer and other Microsoft programs, such as Live Essentials.

Finally, you can find additional accelerators. Just click All Accelerators and Find More Accelerators, as shown here.

Consider the following accelerators:

- Bing Maps
- Share on Facebook
- Bing Translator
- Amazon Search Accelerator
- Find on Facebook
- Define with Wikipedia
- The Weather Channel Accelerator.

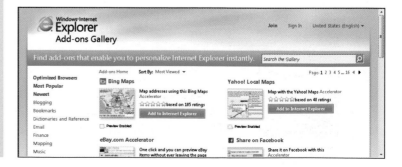

Web slices are a new feature of IE8. Using web slices, you can stay up to date without having to manually check frequently changing data such as the weather, sports scores, traffic or new email. If a web slice is available on a web page, a green web slice icon will appear on the Command bar. (Alternatively, you may see an orange RSS feed, detailed in the next section.) Clicking the green web slice icon lets you see what slices are available and allows you to subscribe to them. Once subscribed, when new information becomes available, the web slice will be highlighted, pointing out that the information on the page has changed (the weather is taking a turn for the worse or there's a new traffic jam). Web slices are becoming more and more popular, and offer a convenient way to keep up with ever-changing web pages, specifically those with bid information, weather, email, stocks, etc.

◀ Work with web slices

Using web slices

1 Locate a web page that offers web slices. Try *www.cnn.com*.

2 Locate the green web slice icon on the Command bar and click it.

3 To add the web slices for the page, click Add to Favorites Bar.

4 Note the new items on the Favorites bar.

7

? Did you know?

When there's something new on the web slice you haven't seen, it darkens. After you click it, it lightens.

Use RSS

So far you've been browsing the web by manually typing in web addresses, clicking links and going from site to site to find the information you want. There's a new way to access information on the Internet, though, and it's called RSS, or Really Simple Syndication (and occasionally Rich Site Summary). RSS is a new technology that is used for issuing news and other web-based content via the Internet, and is being offered by more and more websites each day. RSS content is offered to users in RSS format, and you can access that content using IE8.

Here's how it works. Say you visit a website such as *www. microsoft.com* and read the latest company news and information. The next time you visit the site you will see some of that material again and you'll have to wade through it to access information you have yet to see, or information that's been recently added. What RSS feeds do is let you 'subscribe' to RSS data. The feed you subscribe to will then be updated automatically on your computer when you're online and will acquire only information you've yet to view. When you view the feed, the newest data is listed first and you no longer have to pick through information you've already seen.

To get started with RSS, you'll need to locate the orange Feeds button on the Command bar in IE8. This button will turn orange only when you're visiting a website that offers at least one RSS feed. If it's grey, it's useless – no RSS feeds here. *www.microsoft.com* offers at least one RSS feed and thus, the RSS icon turns orange. Take a look.

To see the available RSS feed for a site, click the arrow next to the orange RSS icon. To subscribe to a feed, click it. You'll be transported to a web page that allows you to subscribe. To complete the process, just click the Subscribe to this feed link.

Microsoft News Center

You are viewing a feed that contains frequently updated content. When you subscribe to a feed, it is added to the Common Feed List. Updated information from the feed is automatically downloaded to your computer and can be viewed in Internet Explorer and other programs. Learn more about feeds.

Subscribe to this feed

4

You'll have the opportunity to name the feed in a familiar window that looks almost exactly like the Favorites window. Just like Favorites, you can create folders and organise feeds similarly. Once you've subscribed, the Feeds view changes to indicate that you've effectively subscribed to the feed. As with Favorites, you access your subscribed feeds through the Favorites Center.

Subscribe to this Feed

Subscribe to this Feed

When you subscribe to a feed, it is automatically added to the Favorites Center and kept up to date.

Name: Microsoft News Center   5

Create in: Feeds ▼   New folder

☐ Add to Favorites Bar

What is a Feed?   Subscribe   Cancel

Subscribing to RSS feeds

1 Browse to a website that offers an RSS feed. Try *www.microsoft.com*, a local newspaper's website, technical sites, or your favourite website.

7

2 When you see an orange RSS icon on the Command bar, click it.

3 Click the feed to subscribe to.

4 Click Subscribe to this feed to subscribe.

5 Type a name for the feed.

6 Use the drop-down list to select an existing folder in which to save the feed, or select New Folder.

7 If you select New Folder, type a name for the folder and click Create.

8 Click Subscribe.

Use RSS (cont.)

Working with RSS feeds

1 Click the yellow star icon to open the Favorites Center.

2 Click Feeds if it isn't already selected.

3 View the feeds by expanding folder names if necessary.

4 To view a feed, select it.

There's a lot going on behind the scenes in IE8, and a lot of it is security-related. There's a pop-up blocker to keep unwanted ads from appearing when you visit web pages configured with them, and there are preconfigured Security Zones and Privacy Settings to help protect against any other threats you may run across while surfing the web. Since much of this is preconfigured, and because general computer security is covered in Chapter 15, we won't go into much detail here regarding those features. However, there are a few things to discuss that aren't automatic, specifically, cleaning up IE by deleting files that can be used to trace where you've been on the Internet. If you share your computer and do not use user accounts to log on and off, you may want to clear your surfing history after each browsing session. You may also want to browse in private if you don't want any data to be saved (thus eliminating the need to erase your browsing history). You can do that with InPrivate Browsing.

Deleting your web footprint

If you don't want people to be able to snoop around on your computer and find out which sites you've been visiting, first create a password-protected user account for yourself (Chapter 15). You should do this anyway since you're using a portable computer. If it's lost or stolen, you want to make it a little more difficult to break into.

If you're worried beyond that, or if you don't always log off when you've finished using the computer (or if you're doing something online you shouldn't be), you'll want to use a new feature called Delete Browsing History. Delete Browsing History is located under the Safety menu.

Delete Browsing History lets you delete the following files:

■ Temporary Internet Files – these are files that have been downloaded and saved in your Temporary Internet Files folder. A snooper could go through these files to see what you've been doing online.

Stay safe online

Important

7

Because you're using a portable computer that can easily be lost or stolen, immediately delete (or do not save) form data such as your name, address and phone number. Similarly, do not save passwords and user names when prompted by IE. If someone steals your computer and gets into your user account, you don't want them to be able to access your personal web data, update your social networking status, check your email, or make purchases from web accounts.

Stay safe online (cont.)

- Cookies – these are small text files that include data that identifies your preferences when you visit particular websites. Cookies are what allow you to visit, say, *www. amazon.com* and be greeted with Hello <your name>, We have recommendations for you! Cookies help a site offer you a personalised web experience.

- History – this is the list of websites you've visited or any web addresses you've typed. Anyone with access to your computer and user account can look at your History list to see where you've been.

- Form data – this is information that's been saved using Internet Explorer's autocomplete form data functionality. If you don't want forms to be filled out automatically by you or someone else who has access to your computer and user account, delete this. Since you're using a portable computer, you should not be saving this data to your computer anyway; you don't want a thief to have access should your computer go missing.

- Passwords – these are passwords that were saved using Internet Explorer's autocomplete password prompts. The same warning applies here as it does to Form data above.

- InPrivate Blocking data – this is data that has been saved to detect where websites may be automatically sharing details about your visit.

!

Important

You also have the option to preserve your Favorites and website data such as cookies and temporary Internet files that you've input and want to keep, for instance those you use at Amazon or other sites you've saved. This will be up to you, but because it's so easy to lose or have a portable computer stolen, we suggest you don't keep this data on your mobile PC.

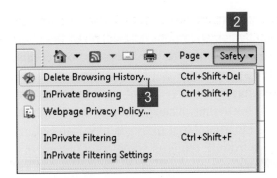

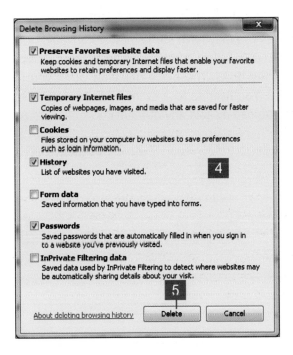

Viewing and clearing History

1 Open Internet Explorer.

2 Click Safety.

3 Click Delete Browsing History.

4 To accept the defaults for all of the listed items, click the Delete button. Otherwise, select and deselect as desired.

5 Click Delete.

Using InPrivate Browsing

1 Click Ctrl + T to open a new tab in IE.

2 Click Open an InPrivate Browsing window.

3 Browse as desired and close the window when finished.

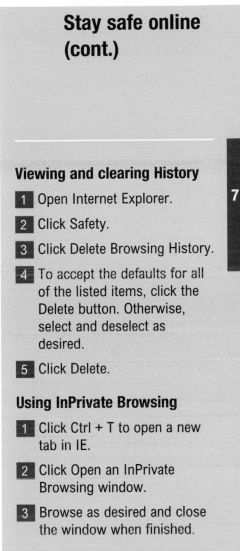

Finally, if you know you're about to go online and look at something you shouldn't, or if you're shopping for birthday or holiday presents and are afraid your kids might be snooping on your computer after you're finished, or if you simply want to browse without leaving any footprint, try InPrivate Browsing.

Get rid of unnecessary add-ons

The two main things that will slow down your Internet browsing activities are a poor connection to the Internet and too many add-ons. You can enhance your connection in many ways: by moving closer to a wireless access point in a building, by having a better line of sight to the satellite offered by your ISP for mobile access, or by connecting to a locate network via Ethernet. Most of this is physical. Getting better performance from IE requires some computer work – you need to disable add-ons you don't use.

Add-ons are easily acquired, and sometimes without your knowledge. You may have some toolbars enabled, for instance, to help you earn miles, access your email, blog, Skype, or perform other tasks. These add-ons slow down your surfing experience. You need to look at the add-ons you have and see whether you can disable any of them.

Disabling unnecessary add-ons

1 Click Tools and click Manage Add-ons.

2 Verify Currently loaded add-ons is selected.

3 If you see something you recognise and don't use, click it and click Disable.

4 It's generally best to leave Microsoft add-ons enabled, including but not limited to:

 a. Microsoft Silverlight

 b. Windows Live ID Sign-in Helper

 c. Search Helper.

5 Click Close when you've finished.

! Important

Some websites require certain add-ons to function properly. Leave items such as Shockwave Flash Object and add-ons related to Java enabled.

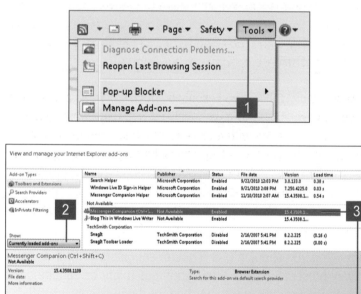

Use Windows Live Essentials

Introduction

Windows 7 doesn't come with an email program, a messaging program or a photo-editing program – you learned that in Chapter 1. You'll probably want to choose programs for these purposes, and we suggest Windows Live Essentials. We've been using it on our netbooks and laptops for a few years, and the programs run well and seem to use very few system resources. You'll also get a free Windows Live ID and some perks you might find too good to be true, such as 25 GB of free Internet storage space when you sign up.

Once you've installed Live Essentials, obtained an ID and signed in, you'll have access to a personalised web page which you can customise, complete with a place to store documents on the web and create your own blog space, among other things. Note that you can choose to install additional applications from the suite, too, including a movie-editing program, a simple program for blogging, and the Internet Explorer toolbar that connects all of this together seamlessly – and It's all free!

What you'll do

Install Windows Live Essentials

Get a Windows Live ID

Log into Windows Live on the Internet

Customise your Windows Live home page

Add a document to SkyDrive

Windows Live Essentials includes the following programs (note that this is not a complete list of Live programs):

- Messenger – instant messaging software you can use to send instant messages to others who you choose as contacts. Messenger contacts are integrated with Mail contacts to make communications easy and simple.

- Mail – a web based email program you can use to send, receive and manage your email. Mail integrates with Messenger and other Live Essentials programs seamlessly. See Chapter 9 for more information.

- Writer – a program that lets you share your photos and videos using blog services such as Windows Live, Wordpress, Blogger, Live Journal and more. A 'blog' is a web log and is generally used to share one's opinions, thoughts and personal information.

- Photo Gallery – a web-based photo-editing and management program that lets you move pictures from your camera to your PC. With Photo Gallery you can edit, share and create panoramic photos. See Chapter 10 for more information.

- Movie Maker – this program lets you create movies from video clips taken from your digital camera or other sources and share them with friends and family via CD, DVD or even the Web.

- Toolbar – this is a toolbar that, after installation, appears in Internet Explorer. The Toolbar integrates access to Mail, Messenger, Photos and more, all from a single place.

- Family Safety – this program helps you keep your family safe from Internet sites that could harm your PC or be inappropriate for viewing. You can configure Family Safety to block websites when your kids log on, allow them (or not) to speak with contacts, and even monitor where your children are going when they are online. Family Safety has to be installed on all PCs your kids use, though, so if you have more than one PC that is something to consider. Unless you have children to protect, I suggest you do not install this program.

Get Windows Live Essentials (cont.)

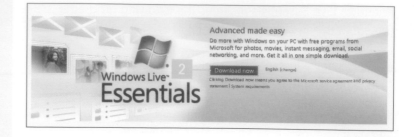

Installing Windows Live Essentials

1 Open Internet Explorer and go to *http://download.live.com*.

2 Click Download now.

3 Click Run.

4 Wait for a few seconds and if prompted, click Yes and/or enter Administrator credentials to continue.

5 Click Choose the programs you want to install.

6 Choose those programs you'll use and no others. (You can always return here if you decide you want additional programs.)

7 Select the programs to install and then click Install.

8 Complete any final installation tasks.

Windows Live Essentials 2011

What do you want to install?

Any existing Windows Live programs will be closed and updated automatically to the latest version.

- Install all of Windows Live Essentials (recommended)
  Windows Live Essentials includes: Messenger, Photo Gallery, Movie Maker, Mail, Writer, Family Safety, Windows Live Mesh, Messenger Companion, Bing Bar, Outlook Connector Pack, and Microsoft Silverlight.

- Choose the programs you want to install

5

By clicking an installation option you agree to the Microsoft service agreement and privacy statement. You will get updates for this and other Microsoft programs from Microsoft Update. This software may also download and install some updates automatically.

Privacy   Service agreement   Learn more

Important

If you're using a netbook, install only the programs you know you'll use. You don't want to fill up your netbook with programs you don't need.

If you've never downloaded and/or installed a program before, you may be a little nervous about doing so. Don't worry, it's really easy, and Microsoft has set it up so that the process requires very little input from you. There are only a few steps: go to the website, click the Download link and wait for the download and installation process to complete.

When you use Live services, such as Live Mail, Live Photo Gallery, Live Messenger and others, you may be prompted to log into them using a Windows Live account. Even if you don't have to log in, we suggest you do. The login credentials are free and you can use them to sign into Live-related websites on the Internet, too. Beyond that, though, by incorporating a Windows Live ID, you can seamlessly connect all of your Live programs for a better computing experience, by making each available from the other.

Getting a Windows Live ID

1 If you have just finished installing Windows Live Essentials you can opt to get a Windows Live ID from the interface. (If not, visit *http://signup.live.com*.)

2 Fill out the required information and click I accept when you've finished.

8

Did you know?

You can use your Windows Live email address and password to log into your Live programs on the Internet and to log into Microsoft websites.

Create your Windows Live ID
It gets you into all Windows Live services—and other places you see
All information is required.

Already using **Hotmail**, **Messenger**, or **Xbox LIVE**? Sign in now

Use your email address: Example: someone@example.com
Or get a Windows Live email address

Create a password:
6-character minimum; case sensitive

Retype password:

First name:

Last name:

Country/region: United States

State: Select one

ZIP code:

Gender: Male Female

Birth year: Example: 1990

Enter the characters you see
New | Audio | Help

Clicking **I accept** means that you agree to the Microsoft service agreement and privacy statement. You also agree to receive email from Windows Live, Bing, and MSN with service updates, special offers, and survey invitations. You can unsubscribe at any time.

Important

Give true information. This is an ID, after all.

Sign in with your new Windows Live ID

Once you've obtained your Windows Live ID, you can log into any of the Live programs you've installed on your computer. You'll be prompted to do this the first time you open any one of them. Logging in will help personalise the programs and will enable you to incorporate your data to your web components easily.

Logging into Windows Live on the Internet

1 Open Internet Explorer and navigate to *http://login.live. com*.

2 Type your new Live ID and password and click Sign In.

3 Hover the cursor over Windows Live, then click Home.

4 Click Photos at the top of the page. Note that you can create an album, add photos, and more.

Did you know?

When you sign up for a Windows Live ID you get a free, personalised web presence (page) on the Internet. You can customise your free web page with your physical location, personal thoughts and pictures, you can upload pictures to folders to share, make and save contacts, communicate with social networking tools, and even store sensitive data.

You can also log into Live services on the Internet. This is really where the fun is! If you haven't done so already, visit *www.login.live.com*, type your user name and password, and click Sign In. Once there, click Windows Live, then Home. You may be surprised at what you find!

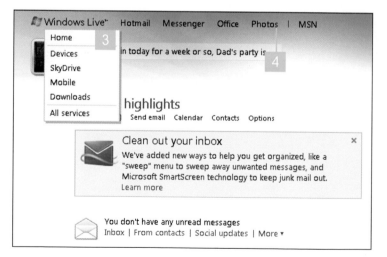

Recent albums on SkyDrive

Here's a great pic!   Quick photos   Downtown Dallas Trip

Messenger social

Greg Blanks ★ shared photos - via Facebook - 9 hours ago
- 2 comments

5 Continue exploring as desired.

8

Personalise your Windows Live home page

You know that along with your free Windows Live ID you get a personalised web page. You can configure the options on the page to suit your needs. For instance, if you input your postcode you'll get personalised weather information. Your page is much more than that, though. If you want to see everything on offer, hover your mouse over the Windows Live option shown earlier and click All Services. Here are just a few of the services you have free and easy access to:

■ Calendar – here you can input events and appointments, check your schedule and to-do list, share calendars with others, and get reminders for upcoming events.

■ Contacts – here you can add, delete and otherwise manage the contacts you acquire via Mail and Messenger. You can even add friends from Facebook and MySpace.

■ Groups – here you can create groups for just about anything, such as a football team or gardening club, and stay connected to them in various ways.

■ Office – use this to view, edit and share Word, Excel, PowerPoint and OneNote documents from anywhere using the Microsoft Office Web apps and SkyDrive.

■ Photos – here you can post your favourite pictures right to your new Live web page, share videos online and create slide shows to share with others. You can choose who to share with, too.

- SkyDrive – here you can save files to the Internet for safe keeping. This is especially useful when using a netbook or laptop, as these are easily stolen. You'll learn later how to access SkyDrive and upload documents to it.

- Spaces – with Spaces you can create yet another, better, larger and more customisable web page to create a blog, post photos, videos, and more. Here is my Spaces page.

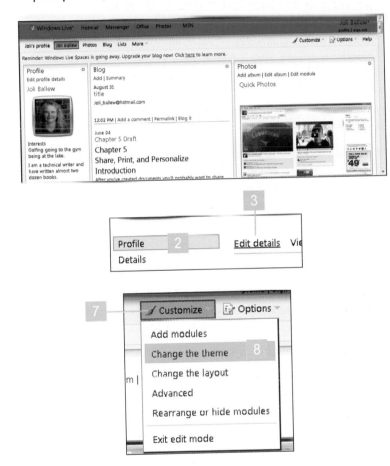

Personalise your Windows Live home page (cont.)

Customising your Windows Live home page

1 Visit *www.login.live.com* and log in using your Windows Live ID.

2 In the top right corner, click Profile.

3 Click Edit details.

4 Click Edit again in any section (Contact Info, Work Info, etc.).

5 Edit as desired and click Save.

6 Click Spaces in the left pane.

7 Click Customize.

8 Choose any option; here, Change the theme is selected.

9 Edit as desired and save changes.

8

For your information

Click Photos at the top of the page to create an album and upload your favourite photos.

Use SkyDrive

SkyDrive is one place on your Windows Live home page you'll want to spend some additional time exploring. You can access SkyDrive from the Windows Live option at the top of the page. As noted earlier, SkyDrive offers a place to store data on Microsoft's Internet services. This keeps the data off your laptop or netbook, but also makes the data available from any computer that offers an Internet connection.

There are many reasons to keep data off of your netbook or laptop, the most important being to secure the data if your computer is lost or stolen and to preserve system resources related to the amount of hard drive space you have. Of course, having the ability to get online and access your documents when you don't have your computer with you is certainly good, too.

Did you know?

SkyDrive offers 25 GB of space to save your data to. That's a lot! Think about it – your entire hard drive may be 80 GB, so 25 GB is quite a luxury.

When you first open SkyDrive, it will be empty. It's up to you to add folders and data. Once you've done that you can opt to share or not to share what you've uploaded. Here you can see some of the folders I've saved to my personal SkyDrive page. The photos I've saved are not shown, but they are available below the Documents section.

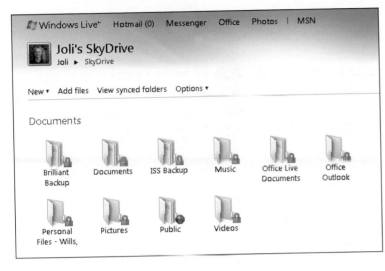

Adding a document to SkyDrive

1 Log into Windows Live.

2 Hover the cursor over Windows Live and click SkyDrive.

3 Click Add files.

4 Click New Folder.

5 Name the folder and click Next.

6 Position this window and an Explorer window so you can drag files from one to the other.

8

Did you know?

You can save your wills, personal directives and other data on SkyDrive and share them with your parents or children. Should something happen, they know where to get the information and can access it from any computer that offers Internet access.

3

Create a folder
Joli ► SkyDrive ► Create a folder

Name: My Sensitive Data —— 5

Share with: Just me Change

[Next] [Cancel]

Use SkyDrive (cont.)

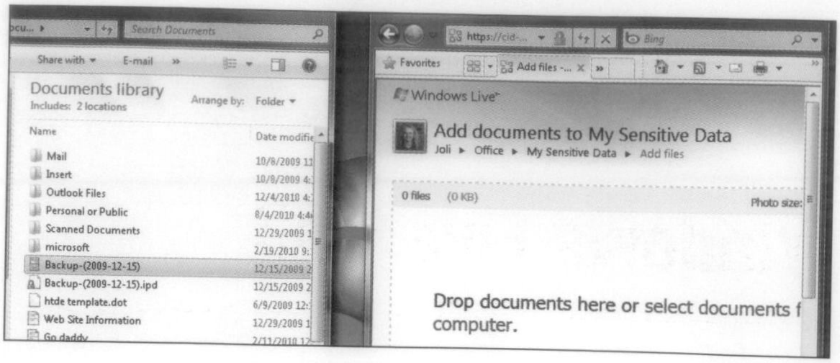

7 Drag any document to add it to SkyDrive.

Windows Live Mail

Introduction

You know that Windows 7 does not come with an email client. Although you can choose from several, including Microsoft Office Outlook, Windows Live Mail is probably all you need. In fact, Windows Live Mail is a better option than many others when using a low-end netbook because it uses very few resources to function and offers lots of features. We also believe that having an email client is better than not having one (and instead, checking your email from an email provider's web page) because you have more control over your email and can manage it any way you like. For all these reasons and more, we've opted to introduce how to use Windows Live Mail, the program we think you should choose for managing email on your laptop or netbook.

What you'll do

Set up an email address

Resolve email set-up errors

View an email and open an attachment

Compose and send an email

Reply to and forward an email

Attach a picture or file using the Insert tab

Add or edit a contact

Configure Windows Live Mail junk email options

Create a folder

Clean Windows Live Mail

> **Important**
>
> The alternative to installing and using an email client is to check your email from your email provider's web mail page. For instance, you can navigate to *www.gmail.com* to check email from your Gmail account, or *www.yahoo.com* to check email from your Yahoo! account. An email client allows you to have more control, though, and to integrate the data on/to your computer more easily.

You can do quite a bit with Windows Live Mail. You can send and receive email, manage your contacts, manage sent, saved and incoming email, and send email that includes photographs and other attachments. Within Windows Live Mail you can also create folders for storing email you want to keep, manage unwanted email, open attachments, and more.

To use Windows Live Mail, you first need to download it. It's part of the Windows Live Essentials suite you learned about in Chapter 8. If you haven't downloaded it yet, return there for instructions. Once Windows Live Mail is installed, you'll need an email address, which you can get from your ISP, Microsoft, Google, Yahoo! and other places. Of course, you can use your Windows Live ID as an email address, too – again, introduced in Chapter 8. Once Live Mail is set up to use your email address(es), you'll be ready to send and receive mail.

Important

In this chapter we'll be using Windows Live Mail 2011. If you have an earlier version, you should consider upgrading.

To use Windows Live Mail you need to set up an email address. This is first and foremost and is done even before exploring the Mail interface. That's because the first time you use Windows Live Mail you'll be prompted to input information regarding your email address. When inputting and configuring your first email address (and any subsequent ones), you'll need to input the following information:

■ Email address – this is where you type the email address you chose when you signed up with your ISP, or when you obtained a free email address from Microsoft, Gmail, Yahoo!, AOL, etc. It often takes this form: *yourname@yourispname. com, yourbusinessname@gmail.com, or yournickname@ yahoo.com.* Email addresses are not case-sensitive.

■ Password – this is where you'll enter the password you chose when setting up your online account with your ISP, Gmail, Yahoo!, Windows Live or other email address provider. Passwords are case sensitive.

■ Display name – this is the name that will appear in the From field when you compose an email and in the sender's Inbox (under From in their email list) when they receive email from you. Don't put your email address here; put your first and last name, and any additional information. I use Joli Ballew, MVP.

Set up an email address

9

Set up an email address (cont.)

Setting up an email address

1 Open Windows Live Mail.

2 You should be prompted to set up an email account automatically. If you aren't (or if you've already created one email account and want to set up a second one):

   a. Click the arrow shown here. This is called the 'Menu icon'.

   b. Click Options.

   c. Click Email accounts.

   d. Click Add.

   e. Click Email Account.

   f. Click Next.

3 Type the required information, but do not tick Manually configure server settings.

Timesaver tip

If you want Windows Live Mail to remember your password, leave Remember this password ticked.

■ Manually configure server settings – this is an option that enables you to type in information about your mail servers. These are settings unique to your specific email provider. Windows Live Mail knows the settings for several email providers, though, so do not check this box when setting up your account. If Windows Live Mail can't find your email provider's settings, you'll be prompted to input them. Usually this includes inputting a POP3 incoming mail server name, an SMTP outgoing mail server name and various authentication settings. If you don't know this information you can call your ISP to ask for it, or you can research it online.

Timesaver tip

When you choose Set an account as the default account, each time you compose a message it will be sent from this account rather than the second or third one.

Configure server settings

If you don't know your email server settings, contact your ISP or network administrator.

Incoming server information

Server type:
POP

Server address: pop.tx.rr.com Port: 110

☐ Requires a secure connection (SSL)

Authenticate using:
Clear text

Logon user name:
joli_ballew@tx.rr.com

Outgoing server information

Server address: smtp.tx.rr.com Port: 25

☐ Requires a secure connection (SSL)
☐ Requires authentication

Cancel Back Next

To test these settings you should send yourself a test email. If you get an error after setting up your email address and sending yourself a test email, read the information carefully. It's probably a typographical error you input during set-up, an error stating that the outgoing server requires authentication (you'll need to tick the appropriate box), or perhaps that the password you typed is incorrect.

4 Click Next. Then:

a. You may be prompted to log in or set the account as the default account, depending on your particular circumstances; you may not. Answer as desired and click Finish.

b. You may be prompted for additional information. Skip to Step 5.

c. If applicable, simply click Finish.

5. If Windows Live Mail prompts you for more information, input it. You will have to call your email provider or search the Internet for the proper settings.

6 Click Next.

7 Click Finish. (If you see errors, refer to the next section.)

8 If this is a second email account, click Close.

Important

Send yourself an email to see whether you can send and receive without errors.

Set up an email address (cont.)

Remember, passwords are case sensitive. Here, the incoming server address was entered incorrectly and is invalid, although that took a bit of sleuthing to figure out.

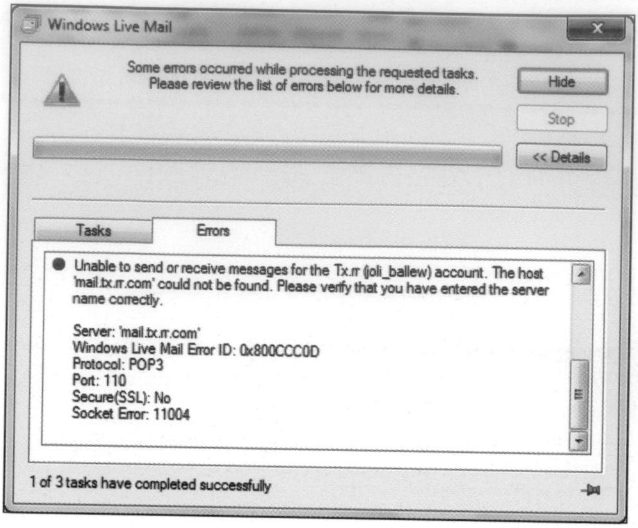

You can resolve errors by editing the properties for an email account. To edit the properties for any account, right-click the account name, as shown here, and click Properties. The Properties dialogue box that opens will allow you to reenter information, including the email address, password, name on the account, outgoing and incoming server names, and more. Here we'll need to change the incoming server name to correct the problem.

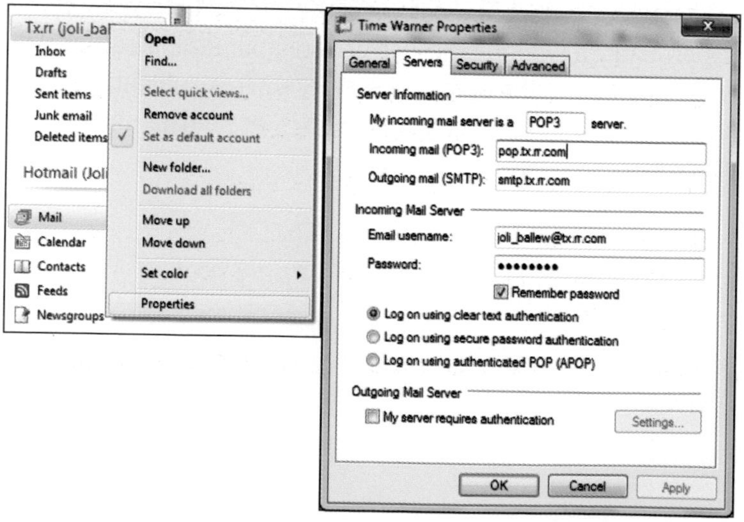

!

Important

Some email servers must complete a process of downloading existing messages to your computer before you can use the email address. If you see a message that messages are being downloaded, let that process complete before you start troubleshooting a connection.

!

Important

If you are repeatedly asked for a password even after inputting it and you do not receive mail after doing so, you will need to review the properties for the account. Something is wrong with the settings for the account.

Now that you have your email address(es) set up, you can explore how Windows Live Mail organises your email in the Folder List pane on the left side of the interface. There are several default folders, and you can add your own if you wish.

- Unread email – this holds email you have yet to read in any other view.

- Unread from contacts – this holds email from known contacts, those in your address book, that you've yet to read.

- Unread feeds – this holds email from feeds you subscribe to. Feeds are content you subscribe to, such as a news source, that offer updated content often.

- Inbox – this folder holds mail you've received.

- Drafts – this folder holds messages you've started but not completed. Click File and click Save to put an email in progress here.

- Sent items – this folder stores copies of messages you've sent.

Resolving email set-up errors

1. Right-click the name of the email address to repair and click Properties.

2. In the Properties dialogue box, browse through the tabs and repair the mistake. When in doubt, call your ISP or email provider (or research the problem on the Internet).

3. Click OK.

4. Send another test email from the account to it. Watch for errors.

9

Set up an email address (cont.)

■ Junk email – this folder holds email that Windows Live Mail thinks is spam. You should check this folder occasionally since Mail may put email in there you want to read.

■ Deleted items – this folder holds mail you've deleted.

■ Outbox – this folder holds mail you've written but have not yet sent.

At the bottom of the Folders pane are view options: Mail, Calendar, Contacts, Feeds and Newsgroups. By default, Mail is selected and is shown here. If you click another option, such as Calendar, the interface changes, also shown.

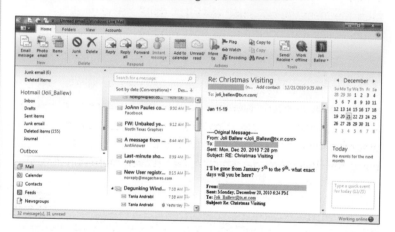

When in Mail view (click Mail in the left corner of Windows Live Mail), each time you click the Send/Receive button, Windows Live Mail checks to see whether you have any new mail on your email server. You can click this button at any time to check for new email; however, by default, Windows Live Mail will check every 10 minutes.

When you receive mail, there are two ways to read it. You can click the message once and read it in the Preview pane, or double-click it to open it in its own window. Most people just click the email once – that way you don't have to close any windows after reading an email (which is what you'd have to do if you double-clicked). However, if your laptop or netbook's screen is really small, you may need to double-click it to see the email effectively. You can also adjust the size of the panes by dragging the grey border between any of them up or down when using the Reading pane, which makes it even more convenient.

For your information

To have Windows Live Mail check for email more often than every 10 minutes (or less often), click the arrow in the top left corner of Live Mail by the Menu icon, click Options and click Mail. From the General tab, change the number of minutes from 10 to something else.

Important

You may see a message that indicates pictures have been blocked to help prevent the sender from identifying that you've opened the message on your computer. You'll have to click the message to download pictures, but do that only if you know the sender and want to see the images.

Read, compose, send and more

Viewing an email and opening an attachment

1. In Windows Live Mail, click the Send/Receive button to check for mail.

2. When new mail arrives, click it once to read it in the Preview pane.

9

Read, compose, send and more (cont.)

3 If the email contains an attachment, you'll see a paperclip icon. You'll also see icons for the attachments in the message itself. If it's something that Windows Mail recognises and can preview, you can opt to view a preview of it in the Preview pane by clicking it once; if not, you'll be prompted to open it.

4 Sometimes you won't be able to open an attachment because you don't have the proper program installed on your computer. When this happens you can ask the sender to resend the file in another format or you can use the Internet to find a program to use.

| chapters | 12/19/2010 |
| morin | |

To: joli_ballew@tx.rr.com;

56903w.doc   56902art.zip

◄◄ ►►

hey Joli, now sending you chapters 2 & 3 of the W7 QuickSteps, will you confirm arrival at your end? You should now have chapters 1-5.

thx.

Mail Attachment

Do you want to open this file?

Name: 56903w.doc
Type: DOC File

3

Open   Cancel

☑ Always ask before opening this type of file

While files from the Internet can be useful, some files can potentially harm your computer. If you do not trust the source, do not open this file. What's the risk?

Windows

Windows can't open this file:

File: 56903w.doc

To open this file, Windows needs to know what program you want to use to open it. Windows can go online to look it up automatically, or you can manually select from a list of programs that are installed on your computer.

What do you want to do?

◉ Use the Web service to find the correct program
○ Select a program from a list of installed programs

4 — OK   Cancel

Compose and send email

You compose an email message by clicking Email message on the toolbar. This icon is located on the Home tab to the far left. (Mail needs to be selected at the bottom of the Folder pane.) The Email message icon and a new mail message are both shown here. Notice that all of the available fields are empty. You will fill them in.

The To line is where you input who the email should be sent to. The Subject line is where you type the subject. The body is where you type the message. Once you click inside the body, features on the Ribbon (that's the blue bar that runs across the top of the Live Mail window) are enabled. This is where you'll access familiar commands such as Cut, Copy and Paste, the option to choose a font, font size, font colour and font style, and access features including Find, Word Count, Attach File, Emoticons, and more.

Here are some things to consider before and while you compose an email:

- You'll need the email address of the recipient; you'll type this into the 'To' field. Alternatively, you can click 'To' to choose the contact from your address book.

- To send the email to more than one person, type their email address and put a semicolon between each entry, like this: *joli@isp.com; bob@microsoft.com; kim@aol.com.* Alternatively, you can select the names from your address book and Live Mail will insert the semicolons automatically.

Composing and sending an email

1 Verify that you're in Mail view, then click Email message.

2 In the 'To' field, type the email address for the recipient. If you want to add names, separate each email address by a semicolon.

3 Type a subject in the 'Subject' field.

4 Type the message in the body pane.

5 Format the text as desired using the formatting tools offered.

6 Click Send.

9

Read, compose, send and more (cont.)

Replying to and forwarding an email

1. Click on an email you've received and click Reply, Reply all or Forward.

2. In the 'To' field, type the email address for the recipient. If you want to add names, separate each email address by a semicolon.

3. Complete the email as desired.

4. Click Send.

- If you want to send the email to someone and you don't need them to respond, you can put them in the Cc line. Cc stands for carbon copy. (You can show this by clicking Show Cc & Bcc.)

- If you want to send the email to someone and you don't want other recipients to know you have included them in the email, add them to the Bcc line. (You can show this by clicking Show Cc & Bcc.) Bcc stands for blind carbon copy and is a secret copy.

- Type the subject of the message in the 'Subject' field. Make sure the subject adequately describes the body of your email. Your recipients should be able to review the subject line later and be able to recall what the email was regarding.

- Type the message in the body of the email. Note that you can edit the data as you would in any word-processing program – you can cut, copy and paste, change the font, and more.

Beyond sending a new email, you can reply to an email or forward an email that you have received. Replying lets you send a response to the sender (you can reply to everyone if there are multiple recipients in the email). Forwarding lets you send the entire email to another person, which is most often used to send an email to someone not included in the email you received. People spend a lot of time forwarding emails, and even though it's common practice, beware. Most forwarded emails contain bad jokes, untrue information (hoaxes), or just unnecessary junk you don't want to read. Do your part by limiting what you forward; just because you think it's true or funny doesn't make it so.

Important

Be careful when you click Reply all. Doing so means your response will go to all the recipients of the original message, including any Cc recipients. (It won't go to blind Cc recipients.) You might mean to tell the sender something private and end up telling everyone your business!

Send an attachment

Although email that contains only a message serves its purpose quite a bit of the time, often you'll want to send a photograph, a short video, a sound recording, a document, or other data. When you want to add something to your message, it's called adding an attachment.

You can use the Insert tab while composing an email message to attach something to it. From there you can click Attach file, Photo album or Single photo to get started. Then, you can browse to the location of the file to attach, which is probably one of your personal folders. As with selecting and deleting multiple files in other scenarios, you can hold down the Ctrl key to select non-contiguous files, or the Shift key to select contiguous ones.

9

Read, compose, send and more (cont.)

Attaching a picture or file using the Insert tab

1 Click Email message (in Mail view from the Home tab).

2 In the New Message window, click Insert.

3 Click Attach file.

4 Browse your computer to locate the item to attach and double-click it.

5 Notice the attachment in the new message.

You can also email from within applications, such as Microsoft Word, the Snipping Tool (included with Windows 7), and others. Generally, you'll find the desired option under the File menu, as a submenu of Send, or from a button located in the top right corner, and a submenu of Send. (This is a perk of having an email client installed on your computer – you can't use this method if you only use the provider's web page to send and receive mail.)

> ### Important
>
> Avoid sending large attachments, especially to people you know have a dial-up modem or those who get email only on a small device such as a BlackBerry, iPhone or mobile PC. A video of your grandkids, cats or kids may take you only 8 seconds to send, but it can bog down a dial-up connection for hours.

There's so much more you can do with Windows Live Mail with regard to attaching files, especially pictures. You can create photo albums, for instance, edit images once you've attached them, create a slide show of images, and more. When you have the time, explore these options. This image shows the tab that will appear when you've attached a photo and selected it in the body of the email.

9

Manage contacts ▶

A Windows Live Mail contact is a data file that holds the information you keep about a person. The contact information can include an email address, mailing address, first and last name, spouse's name, and similar data.

You can easily add data using the tabs offered. For instance, from the Personal tab, you can add a street address, country or region, phone, and other information. You can also input birthdays and anniversaries, among other things.

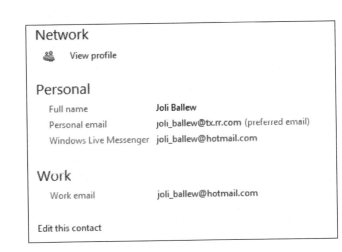

Network

👥 View profile

Personal

Full name   **Joli Ballew**

Personal email   joli_ballew@tx.rr.com (preferred email)

Windows Live Messenger   joli_ballew@hotmail.com

Work

Work email   joli_ballew@hotmail.com

Edit this contact

Adding or editing a contact

1 From Windows Live Mail, click the Contacts icon in the left pane.

2 From the Home tab, click Contact. This will open the Add a Contact window.

3 Type all the information you wish to add. Be sure to add information to each tab.

4 Click Add contact.

5 To edit an existing contact:

    a. In Contacts view, locate the contact.

    b. Click Edit this contact.

    c. Make changes as desired and click Save.

9

Did you know?

From the IM tab, type the contact's Windows Live Messenger address. That way, you'll be able to contact them through Windows Live Messenger – another Live application that's free – to send instant messages.

Deal with unwanted email

▶

Just as you receive unwanted information from radio stations, billboards, television ads, postal mailers and movie theatre ads, you're going to get advertisements in emails. This is referred to as junk email or spam. Unfortunately for you, there's no governing agency placing rules on what can and cannot be sent in an email, as there is with television, radio and other transmission media. This means not only are most of the advertisements scams and rip-offs, they also often contain pornographic images. Even if you were to purchase something via a spam email, it's not guaranteed that the item will arrive or that it will meet any quality requirements. And you can be sure that someone is more interested in having your credit card number than sending you an actual product.

Before you read any further, take note: never – and I mean never – buy anything in a junk email, send money to a sick or dying person, send money for your portion of a lottery ticket, order medication, reply with bank account numbers, National Insurance numbers or any other personal information, believe that Bill Gates himself will pay you for forwarding an email to friends, believe you'll have good luck (or bad) if you don't forward a message to friends, or otherwise do anything but delete the email. Do not attempt to unsubscribe from a mailing list, do not click Reply and do not perpetuate hoaxes.

That said, if you purposefully ask for a legitimate company to send you email, perhaps Amazon.com, it's often OK to click on the link in the email to visit the site. However, always check the web address once you're connected. Just because you click on a link in an email to visit *www.amazon.com* doesn't mean you're going to get there. You might get to a site named *www.1234.amazon.com/validateyourcreditcardnumber*, which would indeed be a scam. It's best to delete all spam.

There are a lot of options for reducing the amount of junk email you receive. First, don't give your email address to any website or company or include it in any registration card unless you're willing to receive junk email from them and their constituents. Understand that companies collect and sell email addresses for profit. Don't get involved in that. Second, keep Mail's junk email options configured as high as you can, and train it to filter unwanted email automatically. With vigilance, you can keep spam to a minimum.

Windows Live Mail helps you avoid unwanted email messages by catching evident junk email and moving it to the Junk email folder. You get to decide how strict Live Mail is, as you'll learn shortly. Additionally, you can block messages from specific email addresses by adding them to the Blocked Senders list and prevent blocking of valid email using the Safe Senders list.

There are four filtering options in Windows Live Mail:

- No Automatic Filtering – use this only if you do not want Windows Live Mail to block junk email messages. Windows Live Mail will continue to block messages from email addresses listed on the Blocked Senders list.

- Low – use this option if you receive very little junk email. You can start here and increase the filter if it becomes necessary.

- High – use this option if you receive a lot of junk email and want to block as much of it as possible. Use this option for children's email accounts. Note that some valid email will probably be blocked, so you'll have to review the Junk email folder occasionally to make sure you aren't missing any email you want to keep.

- Safe List Only – use this option if you only want to receive messages from people or domain names on your Safe Senders list. This is a drastic step and requires you to add every sender you want to receive mail from to the Safe Senders list. Use this as a last resort.

9

Deal with unwanted email (cont.)

Configuring Windows Live Mail junk email options

1 Click the arrow next to the Menu icon (that's the arrow available in the top left corner of Windows Live Mail).

2 Click Options, then Safety options.

3 From the Options tab, make a selection. We suggest starting at High and taking the time to 'train' Live Mail by checking the junk email options often, at least at first, and telling Live Mail when an email is not junk.

4 Click OK.

5 Click the International tab. Read the information offered and decide whether you want to block domains from different countries or encoding lists. Proceed as desired.

6 Click the Phishing tab.

7 Select Protect my Inbox from messages with potential Phishing links. Additionally, move phishing email to the Junk email folder.

Safety Options

| Phishing | Security | Trust Center |
| Options | Safe Senders | Blocked Senders | International |

Windows Live Mail can move messages that appear to be junk email into a special Junk email folder.

Choose the level of junk email protection you want:

○ No Automatic Filtering. Mail from blocked senders is still moved to the Junk Email folder.

○ Low: Move the most obvious junk email to the Junk Email folder.

3 ● High: Most junk email is caught, but some regular mail may be caught as well. Check your Junk Email folder often.

○ Safe List Only: Only mail from people or domains on your Safe Senders List will be delivered to your Inbox.

☐ Permanently delete suspected junk email instead of moving it to the Junk Email folder

☐ Report junk email to Microsoft and its partners (recommended)

[OK] [Cancel] [Apply]

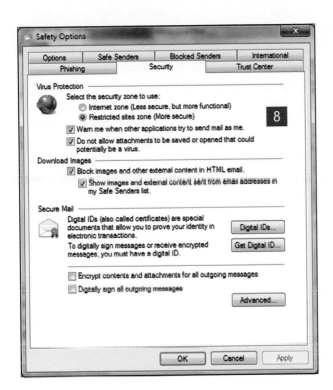

8 Click the Security tab. The default settings are usually fine, but read through them to see whether you'd like to make changes.

9 Click OK.

For your information

On the Security tab, you may want to select Internet zone (Less secure, but more functional) for a better web experience.

9

Keep Live Mail clean and tidy

It's important to perform some housekeeping chores once a month or so. If you don't, you may find it hard to manage the email you want to keep and to find email when you need to access it again – if every email you want to keep is still in your Inbox, you probably have a long list to sift through. That said, we'll end this chapter with three tasks: creating a folder to hold email you want to keep and moving mail into it, and deleting items in the Sent items and Deleted items folders.

Creating a folder

1 In Windows Live Mail, in Mail view, click the Folders tab.

2 Click New folder.

3 Type a name for the new folder.

4 If you have more than one email account configured, in the list, select which Inbox you'd like the folder to be under.

5 Click OK.

Timesaver tip

Create a folder for things you want to keep separate from everything else, for instance Funny Jokes, Videos or Work.

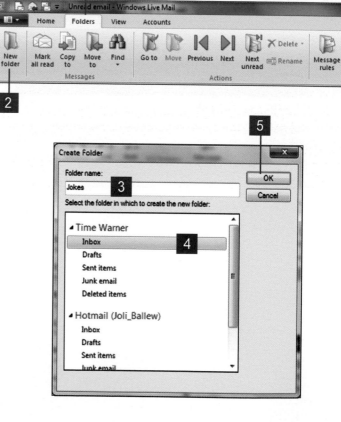

```
▲ Time Warner
  ▲ Inbox (67)
      Jokes          [6]
      Drafts
      Sent items
      Junk email (7)
```

Did you know?

Using the same technique, you can create subfolders inside folders you have created.

```
folder    all read
                        Open
                        Empty 'Junk email' folder   [2]
Quick views             Find...
   Unread email
   Unread from          Mark all as read      Ctrl+Shift+A
   Unread feeds         New folder...
                        Rename...
Time Warne              Delete                Ctrl+Shift+D
   Inbox (67)
     Jokes              Add to compact view
   Drafts               Set color                         ▶
   Sent items           Properties
[1] Junk email (7)              ✕  ▾      Terribles Car Wa
```

Keep Live Mail clean and tidy (cont.)

[6] Note the new folder in the Local Folders list.

[7] To move any email message to the new folder, select it (you probably have to click Inbox first) and drag it to the new folder. Drop it to complete the move.

Cleaning Windows Live Mail

[1] Right-click Junk email.

[2] Click Empty 'Junk email' folder.

[3] Right-click Deleted items.

[4] Click Empty 'Deleted items' folder.

9

Windows Live Photo Gallery

Introduction

Windows 7 does not come with any photo-editing software. It comes with Paint, but that isn't really the type of program you use for uploading, editing, managing and sharing pictures. There is another option, though. Throughout this book we've talked quite a bit about the Windows Live Essentials suite of applications. You may recall that one of those applications, designed to use few resources, work well with Windows 7, incorporate other Live applications and integrate easily with Mail, is Windows Live Photo Gallery. Because it offers so many features, Windows Live Photo Gallery may be all you need to manage, manipulate, view and share your digital photos. So, before you install additional software, including software that was included on the CD that came with your digital camera or printer, or before you pay for any other third-party software, try this free program.

For your information

The Windows Live Essentials suite is not included with Windows 7 – it must be downloaded and installed. If you haven't done that yet, refer to Chapter 8. Make sure you get the 2011 version (or later).

What you'll do

Explore the Photo Gallery Interface

Import pictures

View single pictures or a slide show

Adjust image quality

Crop photos

Tag photos

Share photos and videos

Manage photo and video files

Explore the interface

The first time you open Windows Live Photo Gallery, you'll notice that it has two default panes, and each offers specific functionality. The pane to the left is the View pane, where you'll select the folder or subfolder that contains the pictures you want to view, manage, edit or share. The Thumbnail pane is on the right and this is where you preview the pictures in the folder selected in the View pane. You may not have very many pictures or videos yet.

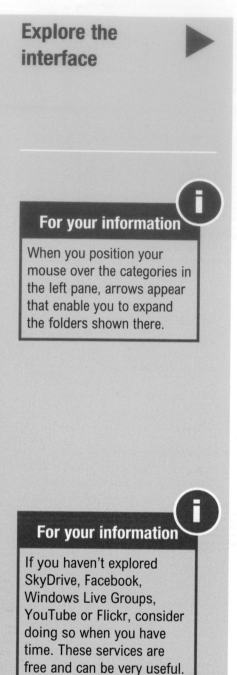

For your information

When you position your mouse over the categories in the left pane, arrows appear that enable you to expand the folders shown there.

For your information

If you haven't explored SkyDrive, Facebook, Windows Live Groups, YouTube or Flickr, consider doing so when you have time. These services are free and can be very useful.

You'll also see the Ribbon. This is the blue bar that runs across the top of the interface. The tools you'll use to edit, enhance, share and perform tasks with photos and videos are located there. For now, look through the items shown on the Home tab, then click the Edit tab, the Find tab, the Create tab and the View tab to see what else is available. The Create tab is shown here. Notice options to set the selected picture as the Desktop picture, order prints, send the picture in an email, and even publish the picture on SkyDrive, Facebook, YouTube, Flickr and Windows Live Groups.

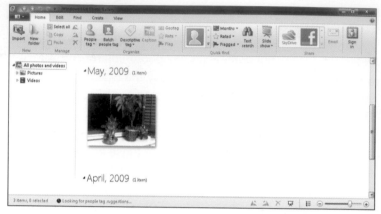

When you double-click a picture in the Thumbnail pane, it opens in a new frame where you can then edit, share, add tags and perform other image-related tasks. Note that when you double-click an image, the left pane disappears and a new pane appears on the right. From that new pane, you can perform common editing tasks quickly.

You can click the tabs on the Ribbon to access additional tools. You can adjust the exposure and colour, for instance, or crop or straighten the photo, among other things. Click the Edit tab, the Create tab and the View tab to see what's available.

Now take a look at the bottom of the Photo Gallery window. The slider allows you to zoom in on the selected photo. Zooming is a great way to get to an area of an image to fix, especially if it's a small area, such as red eye. Moving to the left from the slider there are other navigational controls: a toggle switch to move from the image's actual size to fit to screen, Play slide show (to play a slide show of the folder's pictures), a Delete button, options to rotate right or left, and arrows for Next (to move to the next picture in the folder) and Previous (to move to the previous picture in the folder).

10

Explore the interface (cont.)

Exploring the Photo Gallery Interface

1 Click Start and click All Programs.

2 Click Windows Photo Gallery.

3 Click the down arrow by Pictures in the left pane. You'll have to move your mouse over for this arrow to appear.

4 Navigate to any picture and click it once.

5 At the bottom of the interface, use the slider to change the thumbnail size of the photos in the folder.

6 If you wish, use the buttons to the left of the slider to rotate the picture.

7 From the Home tab, click the arrow next to Rate and apply a rating.

8 From the Home tab, click Sign in.

9 Input your Windows Live ID and password. (If you wish, click Sign me in automatically.)

10 Click Sign in. (You can now more easily integrate Live Photo Gallery with other Live applications.)

170

Did you know?

The next time you want to open Windows Live Photo Gallery, look on the Start menu: it just might be there!

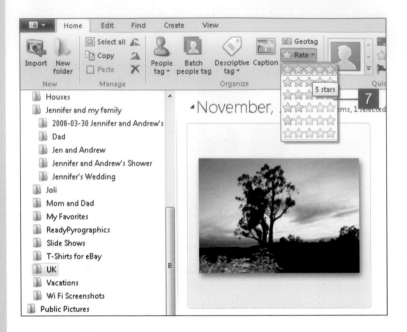

Although you can explore the interface with only a handful of pictures or by viewing the sample pictures that come with Windows 7, before you can do much with Photo Gallery you'll need to import some of your own digital photos. If you have a digital camera, mobile phone, SD card with images on it or some other device that contains photos, you can import the photos from that device into Photo Gallery.

There are lots of different hardware options for taking digital pictures, including mobile phones, smart phones, digital cameras, webcams and video cameras. There are even more ways to store and carry pictures with you, including USB drives, music players, and iPods and iPhones. Finally, there are multiple ways to get pictures onto a computer, including connecting digital cameras, inserting media cards, even obtaining images from scanners. You can even email pictures from a phone (or other device) to your computer! When you connect a digital camera, media card or other device (such as a USB flash drive) that contains pictures, you'll be prompted to select a way to import them. You may see multiple options, as shown here.

How you opt to import pictures and videos is up to you. We actually prefer to open the folder to view the files, then drag and drop the pictures we want to keep from that window to the appropriate folder or subfolder on the computer. The other options can be finicky and may not import what you want where you want it.

10

Import pictures and video (cont.)

Importing pictures using Windows Live Photo Gallery

1 Connect the device. If applicable, turn it on.

2 When prompted, choose Import pictures and videos using Windows Live Photo Gallery.

3 Click Import all new items now and type a descriptive name for the group of pictures you're importing. (Later, you can try the other option, Review, organize, and group items to import.)

4 Click Import.

Here, we're dragging two images from an SD card to a folder on a netbook named Dad's 90th Birthday Party. This way we know the pictures will go right where we want them to go and we won't have to spend time later organising the photos we're importing.

Since you're new to Windows Live Photo Gallery, though, you should give the option Import pictures and videos using Windows Live Photo Gallery a chance. Follow the instructions offered here to do that. If you decide you don't like it, you can always opt for another option.

5 If desired, lick Erase after importing. This will cause Windows 7 to erase the images from the device after the import is complete.

6 Windows Live Photo Gallery will open and you can view the pictures.

Viewing single pictures or a slide show

1 Position your mouse in the left pane over Pictures.

2 Click the arrow beside pictures to see your subfolders.

3 Navigate the folders to locate the pictures to view.

Windows 7 won't recognise all devices, but it does a pretty good job. In fact, it will import pictures from many kinds of mobile phones, including the iPhone. However, on the slim chance your device isn't immediately recognised, you can click the Menu button (located in the top left corner) and click Import pictures and videos, and you'll be given access to additional devices attached to your PC, even scanners.

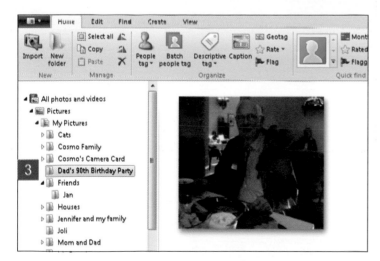

10

Import pictures and video (cont.)

4 To play a slide show of pictures in a folder, select the folder.

5 Click the arrow beside Slide show from the Home tab.

6 Choose a transitioning option.

7 Watch the slide show and move the mouse to see the controls shown here.

8 Click Esc at any time to access controls.

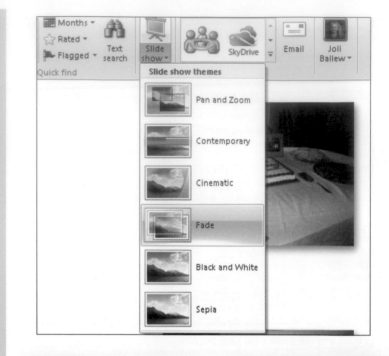

The best way to edit a photo in Windows Live Photo Gallery is to double-click it. When you do, a new view opens offering access to the tools you'll need to adjust the quality of the image and apply effects. From the Ribbon's Edit tab, note these editing options. They are the options you'll use most.

- Auto adjust – this tool automatically assesses the image and alters it, which most of the time results in a better image. However, there's always the Undo button and you'll probably use it on occasion. (The Undo button is on the Quick Access toolbar, at the very top of the interface.)

- Exposure – this tool offers controls for brightness and contrast.

- Color – this tool offers controls to adjust the temperature, tint and saturation of the photo.

- Straighten – this tool automatically straightens photos and offers a slider you can use as well.

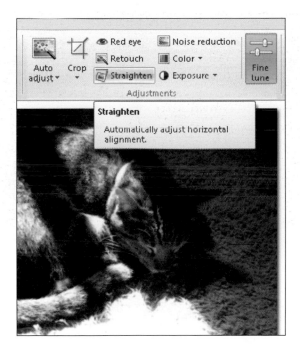

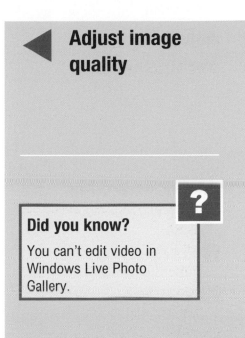

Did you know?

You can't edit video in Windows Live Photo Gallery.

10

- Crop – this tool remove parts of a picture you don't want.

- Red eye – this lets you draw a rectangle around any eye that has a red dot in it and the red dot is automatically removed.

Adjust image quality (cont.)

Adjusting image quality

1. Open Windows Live Photo Gallery.

2. In the View pane, select any folder that contains pictures.

3. Position the zoom slider so you can see several images at once.

4. Double-click a picture to edit. (It's best not to use the Sample Pictures, they're already optimised.)

5. Explore each of the options outlined in the bulleted list, including Red eye, Auto adjust, Color, and more.

6. At any time, click Undo to revert to a previous quality.

7. Click Close file and OK when finished.

Cropping photos

1. Double-click any picture to crop.

2. Click the Crop icon (not the arrow beneath it).

3. Position the crop box as desired, by dragging from its corners.

4. Click the Crop button again to apply.

Additionally, note the options in the pane on the right side of the interface. There are quick links to Adjust exposure, Adjust color, Straighten photo and Adjust detail. (Adjust detail lets you sharpen the image or reduce noise.)

?

Did you know?

At any time you can click Close file on the Ribbon to return to the Windows Live Photo Gallery default interface. If you've made changes, they'll be saved automatically.

If you've worked much with Facebook or any other social networking application, you probably have an idea what tags are. Basically, a tag offers a way to call out a person in a picture without actually writing anything on the picture or changing the picture name (or adding a comment). For Facebook, at least, when you hover your mouse over a picture that's been tagged, the tag will appear. (Move your mouse away and the tag disappears.)

Joli Ballew

You can apply tags to your pictures in Windows Live Photo Gallery, too, but you can do much more than tag a single person or a group. You can tag a photo with an event name, group name, a city or country name, a holiday name, and more.

Tags can be extremely useful when it comes to organising your photos. Once added, tags can be used to group pictures in useful ways. For instance, you can group all photos tagged as 'Italy' to view pictures that are related to a trip you took to Italy. Further, you can group all photos with a single person tagged to view only pictures of that person.

Some tags are applied automatically when you import pictures from a digital camera, including the date they were uploaded, along with any name you applied to the imported group. While the date is important, tagging a photo (or a group of photos) with a label such as Wedding, Cat, Italy trip or similar is a great addition.

10

Did you know?

A single picture can have multiple tags. You might tag a photo as Holiday but also apply tags that name the people in the picture, the city or the country.

Tag photos (cont.)

Tagging photos

1 Open Windows Live Photo Gallery.

2 Locate a picture to tag.

3 Right-click the picture and click Properties.

There are lots of ways to tag photos. It would require too much space to describe them all here. You can right-click a photo and click Properties, for instance, and you can click the Descriptive tab on the Home tab. Additionally, if you've signed into Windows Live Photo Gallery using your Windows Live ID, and if you have lots of contacts, you have even more ways to incorporate tags (using those contacts). You can even 'batch tag' people – that's shown here. We encourage you to explore all tagging options; here we'll just get you started with the basics.

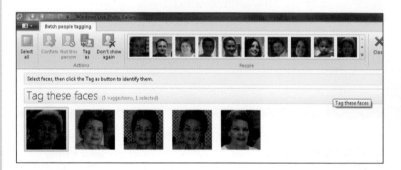

The more people you tag, the more Windows Live Photo Gallery learns. In fact, when you're browsing through tagged photos, you'll be prompted to confirm a person is who Windows Live Photo Gallery thinks it is. It can match faces to faces, and make pretty good guesses, too!

4 Next to tags, type the tag name. If a tag already exists, you can click it in the list.

5 Click OK.

Once you've tagged people and added tags for events and locations, you can sort photos with the new tags. From the Home tab, note the Quick find group. Click any person in the group to view pictures that contain that person. When you do, you may be prompted to confirm that other photos can also be tagged.

10

Tag photos (cont.)

There's so much more you can do with tags, so it's difficult for us to move on without feeling a little bit guilty. We'd like to encourage you to spend some time tagging, though. To continue exploring now, click the arrow by Top people in the Quick find area from the Home tab, and click Not tagged or detected. You can then tag pictures by their location on earth (geotag) or a description (descriptive tag). For the former, choose a physical location such as a city or country name; for a description, choose an event or holiday.

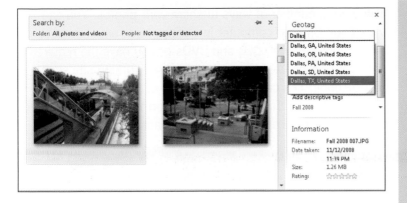

Did you know?

You can tag videos, too. However, since you can't edit videos in Windows Live Photo Gallery, we've opted to leave videos out.

10

Share photos and videos ▶

There are a number of ways to share your photos. You can view them on your computer in a slide show, email them to others, burn them to CDs and DVDs (if you have the required hardware), even post them to a social networking site such as Facebook. You can do just about all of this from Photo Gallery's Create tab. You can also perform some of these tasks with videos. You can upload video to Facebook, for instance, tag videos, and email video to others, provided the video file isn't too large.

Emailing pictures

1 Open Windows Photo Gallery.

2 Select pictures to email. (Hold down the Ctrl key to select non-contiguous pictures or the Shift key to select contiguous ones.)

3 Click the Create tab.

4 Click Email.

5 Choose a picture size (noting the final file size – try to keep the attachment under 4 MB).

6 Click Attach.

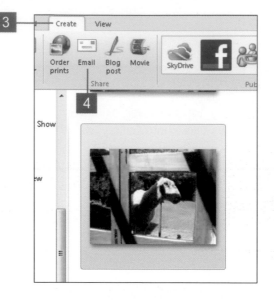

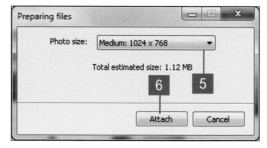

! Important

We're assuming you're using Windows Live Mail.

7 If desired, in Windows Live Mail, click Change to photo album. When you do, the pictures are inserted into the body of the email and you can type captions or add more photos. Here's an example.

8 Complete the email and click Send. (Note that you can click the paperclip icon to revert to attachments if you don't like the Photo Album.)

Uploading pictures to Facebook

1 Select a photo or a group of photos to upload. You can also choose a video.

2 From the Create tab, click the Facebook icon.

3 If prompted to connect to Facebook or create an associate between Live Photo Gallery and Facebook, do so.

4 If applicable, select an existing album or opt to create a new one.

5 As applicable, type a comment or album name.

6 Click Publish.

7 Click View if you'd like to view your photos on Facebook now. Otherwise, click Close.

10

Manage photo files

You can manage your photo and video files from your Photo and Video libraries in Windows 7. You'll see the same folders there you see in Windows Live Photo Gallery. Thus, when you need to create folders, delete pictures, rename pictures or organise pictures into subcategories, it's just as easy to do it in your default folders as it is to do it in Photo Gallery. (In fact, it may well be easier.) We'll suggest, then, that when you need to organise and manage your photo files, you do it in these Windows default folders.

The managing tasks you'll save for Photo Gallery should involve things you can't do in those folders (or can't do as easily), including tagging, uploading to social networking websites and viewing photos in various configurations. As you can see here, we're viewing our pictures by 'person'. You can also sort images by whether they were published (vs. not published), by their date, by their rating, by tags, and more.

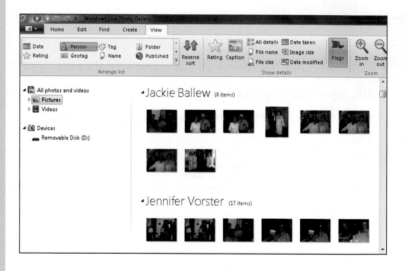

As with the default folders, it's easy to create a folder to manage your photos. You can then drag and drop pictures into it, just as you can in libraries. From the Home tab, select New folder to get started. When you create a folder in Photo Gallery, it also appears in the My Pictures folder on your computer.

You can also choose commands such as Select all, Copy, Paste and more to manage your photos and videos. You can access these commands from the Home tab. This enables you to easily select and then move (or copy) media to another folder.

However you decide to manage your photos, there are a few things to keep in mind:

- Delete photos and videos you don't want.

- Delete duplicate photos and videos.

- Rename photos and videos so you know what they are.

- Add tags to photos and videos.

- Resize large pictures so they take up less space on your hard drive.

Managing your photos and videos

1 Right-click photos and videos to delete them.

2 Right-click photos to resize them.

3 Right-click photos to rename them.

4 Right-click photos and click Properties to tag them.

10

Video messaging with Windows Live Messenger

Introduction

Netbooks and laptops almost always come with webcams. Hence, we're devoting an entire chapter to communicating with them. Confusion often arises with webcams because you can see the lens on the outside of the laptop, you can see the webcam in the Devices and Printers window, and often you can access the webcam and see yourself on it by double-clicking its icon, but you can't use it.

You can't use your webcam in the manner you'd like because the camera does not come with a program for communicating with others through it! You can't just 'turn on' your webcam and send a video stream of yourself to anyone you want to. You have to research what program you want to use to do this, download and install it, add contacts you want to communicate by video with, and only then can you communicate with it. To complicate matters, the people you communicate with via the webcam must agree to use the same program (or one that's compatible with yours) and they must add you as a contact (just as you must add them). It's a bit of a set-up.

In this chapter we'll introduce one option for using your webcam, Windows Live Messenger. As you can probably guess by now, this program is part of the Windows Live Essentials suite of free applications. You have probably already tried Live Mail and Live Photo Gallery, so adding Live Messenger won't be a big move. There are other programs to choose from, though. One very popular video-messaging program is Skype. If you have contacts who rely solely on Skype and you want to communicate with them using video and voice, you will need to obtain both programs.

A webcam is a piece of computer hardware that is included on almost all netbooks and laptops. It lets you transmit live video of yourself to others with whom you specifically choose to video chat. As noted, you can't just send a live video stream to someone; they have to agree to view it! (Can you imagine the uproar that would ensue if someone was able to send you live pictures using their personal live webcam?) Anyway, this type of video communication is often called video messaging or video chatting. In a business environment, the term is video conferencing.

Before you can proceed, you need to verify you have a working webcam. If you know that you have a built-in webcam (and that it works), you can skip this section. However, if you aren't sure, there are several ways to find out.

If you discover you do not have a webcam, you can purchase a small, portable webcam that snaps on to your laptop's lid. They are inexpensive and easy to install and are something to consider if you want to video chat but don't have a camera.

Discovering your webcam

1 Read the information on the outside of the box or in the User Guide that came with your computer. If you have a webcam, it'll say so there.

2 Look for a very small lens above the computer screen. It's probably round and located in the middle and just above the top of the laptop's screen.

3 Click Start and click Devices and Printers. You should see it there.

4 In Control Panel, click View devices and printers.

5 Double-click the webcam icon to see whether it has an associated program to let you test it.

?

Did you know?

Some mobile computers offer a program that allows you to enable the webcam and view yourself in it. You may have access to this program on the Desktop or in the All Programs menu.

Open and sign into Windows Live Messenger

Opening and signing into Windows Live Messenger

1. Click Start, click All Programs and click Windows Live Messenger.

2. Log in if prompted, using your Windows Live ID (see Chapter 8).

3. If prompted to take a new photo, click Take photo or click Skip.

Your netbook or laptop may have come with its own webcam application, but you still need to download and install a messaging program such as Skype, Windows Live Messenger, Yahoo! Messenger, Google Talk, or something compatible. You need a program that you can use to send your video stream to others. Additionally, the people you want to send live video to must have the same program (or one that is compatible with yours) to receive it. So, before deciding on a particular program, ask the people you wish to video chat with what program they use. If they all use, say, Google Talk, and no one uses Live Messenger, then there's no need to get it or spend time configuring it. However, we've found that most people keep several messaging programs on their computers, and will often say, 'I use Google Talk, Windows Live Messenger, and Yahoo! Messenger, so pick whatever suits you', in which case, we suggest you opt for Windows Live Messenger.

> ### Important
>
> You have to download and install Windows Live Messenger before you can use it. Refer to Chapter 8 if necessary.

Welcome to the new Messenger

Stay in touch with the people you care about most with chat, photos and video messages.
See your favorite friends, social highlights, and news headlines - all in one window. Where
do you want to start?

Social Highlights   MSN

msn

There's a chance that you may, fairly immediately, get an instant message text from someone already in your contact list who saw you 'log in' to Windows Live Messenger. If you've incorporated other services, such as Facebook, you may receive messages that others are logging on to services they use as well. If this happens and it is unnerving, from the File menu click Status, then click Appear offline. You can always go back 'online' when you're ready to let the world know you're available.

4 You can connect social services if desired. For now, click Close.

5 Wait while Windows Live Messenger restarts.

Windows Live Messenger

File   Contacts   Actions   Tools   Help

Sign in as joli_ballew@hotmail.com
Sign out
Exit Messenger

Status   ▸   ● Available
                                                     Busy
Go To   ▸   Away
                                                     Appear offline
Send a file...
Open received files folder
View message history...

h with the people you ca
See your favorite friends, social high
do you want to start?

Set up audio and video devices

You may feel that your webcam and audio devices are configured and running properly, but it's still best to work through the set-up processes. This introduces Windows Live Mail to your webcam, microphone and speakers, and enables you to configure preferences, sound levels and playback levels. If applicable, you can select a specific webcam, specific speakers or a specific microphone, which may come into play if you use a headset, for instance. Whatever the case, you should work through the wizard.

Setting up video and audio devices

1. Click Tools and click Set up audio and video devices.

2. Under Speaker, click the Test button to see the volume at which your speakers are configured. Move the slider left or right to reconfigure as desired.

3. Speak normally, from the distance you will normally be sitting from the microphone.

4. Under Microphone, notice the bar that moves when you speak. Move the slider to the left or right so that when you speak you see the green bar move, and when you speak loudly the slider moves into the yellow zone. It should not be in the red zone.

5. Click Next.

For your information

If the speakers or microphone aren't working, try another option under the device's dropdown list. The device that you'll use may not be selected.

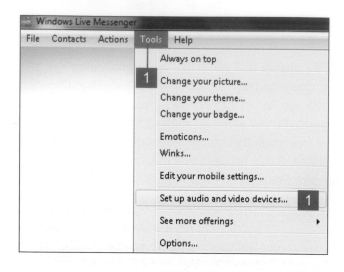

192

Properties

Video Proc Amp | Camera Control

		Auto
Brightness	106	☐
Contrast	71	☐
Hue	7	☐
Saturation	106	☐
Sharpness	7	☐
Gamma	30	☐
White Balance		☐
Backlight Comp	1	☐
Gain		☐

ColorEnable ☐   PowerLine Frequency   60 Hz ▼
(Anti Flicker)

Default

8

OK   Cancel   Apply

Set up audio and video devices (cont.)

11

6 Click Webcam settings.

7 Change the settings as desired. You'll see the change in the webcam window as you move the sliders.

8 Click Apply or Cancel.

9 Click Finish.

For your information

While you're finishing up these configuration tasks, send an email to the person you most wish to communicate with using your webcam. Tell them you've installed and configured Windows Live Mail and will now attempt to add them as a contact. Ask for their Windows Live ID if you like – it'll make adding them easier.

Add a contact

In order to video and voice chat with someone, you have to add them as a contact and they in turn must agree and add you. You need contacts in a contact list. If you don't see any contacts, you haven't added any! There are lots of ways to add contacts. If you use any social networking sites, setting up Social Highlights is a great way to get started. You can also add contacts one at a time, manually.

If you see the Welcome to the new Messenger page shown here and you want to add your social networking contacts, click Social Highlights. Perform any steps required to add your social networking sites, including adding user names and passwords as directed. When you do this, you'll get updates through the Live Messenger window, along with other communication options. (If you don't want to do this, click the MSN link.)

When you've finished, under the Friends section and under add, click Add people from other services. Continue adding contacts using your social networking sites if desired. Here you can see it's possible to add contacts from Facebook, MySpace, LinkedIn, AOL, and more. Note that just because you add these contacts doesn't mean you can automatically video chat with them. Your contacts must have the required software, for one, be logged in and using it, for another, and meet various other requirements listed later in this chapter.

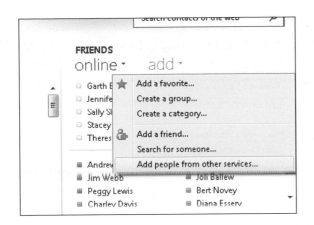

Add people from other services

Facebook

MySpace

LinkedIn

AOL Mail

Hyves

Gmail™

Hi5

Tagged

Outlook

Another Windows Live account

For your information

When you add your social contacts your Windows Live Messenger window offers their updates and various ways to contact them.

When you have a contact you've already decided to video chat with, specifically a contact who also uses Windows Live Messenger and is ready to video chat with you, you can add them using the Contacts menu. Once you've done that, you have to wait for your new contact to log on with their Live ID and accept your invitation.

Add a contact (cont.)

Adding a contact

1 Click Contacts.

2 Click Add a contact.

3 Enter the friend's email address.

4 Click Next.

5 If you wish, tick Make this person a favorite. Click Next.

6 Click Close.

Windows Live Messenger

Add a friend

3

Enter your friend's email address:

PicoandLucy@hotmail.com

Search for people | Add people from other services

Enter a mobile phone number (optional):

Select the country or region

4 — Next   Cancel

Important

We want to make it clear that it's possible to have webcam video conversations with people who aren't using the same program you're using. There are programs that allow this. However, when two people use the same program, there's much less chance that problems will occur.

Although we've talked a bit about personalising the Windows Live Messenger window with social networking contacts, among other things, the purpose of this chapter is still a simple one: you want to have a video and voice conversation with a specific person. The easiest way to do this is for you and this person to obtain and install Windows Live Messenger, log in with a Windows Live ID, then add each other as contacts. Once that's done, any time you are both online and logged in with Live Messenger, you can communicate with video.

Here's a brief summary along with a few caveats for this type of communication:

- Both you and your contact need to be logged into Windows Live Messenger at the same time on your respective computers. One can use a compatible program, although we don't recommend it.

- Each person needs to have accepted the other as a contact.

- One person needs to 'call' the other to get started, and the other person has to 'answer'.

- Both people do not need to have a webcam. One person can send video and the other can send instant messages.

- Ethernet is faster than Wi-Fi and may produce a better connection. If you have problems, consider connecting physically to a router.

- You can have a video conversation with only one person at a time.

- Some older computers can't send and receive video data at the same time, or there's another problem such as lack of bandwidth. Understand that if your contact has an old computer or is on dial-up, you may not both be able to use your webcams at the same time.

Have a video conversation (cont.)

Initiating a video call

1 Verify previously listed requirements are met (you and your contact are logged on and signed into Live Messenger, among other things).

2 Click Actions.

3 Click Video.

4 Click Start a video call.

5 Choose your contact from the list and click OK.

6 Your contact will receive a notification like this one and will have to accept your call. If they do not accept your call, you cannot initiate the video chat.

7 Congratulations! You are now in a video call! Click End call when you've finished.

The Skype messaging program stands out above the others, mainly because it's extremely easy to use, lots of people have it and video calls are free. Like other messaging programs, though, your contacts need to have it, too. So if you're thinking of getting Skype, make sure you have a contact or two who use it as well. To explore Skype, visit *www.skype.com*. Some of the features are shown here.

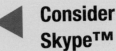

If you decide Skype is something you'd like to try, click the Get Skype link and set up a user name and password. Then, as with Windows Live Messenger, add contacts, wait for them to respond and then initiate a video call.

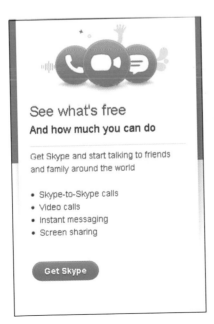

Windows Media Player and Media Center

Introduction

Windows 7 offers two programs for working with and viewing media on your netbook or laptop: Windows Media Player and Windows Media Center. Both enable you to listen to music, view pictures, watch movies and videos and perform other media-related tasks, but each has a vastly different interface. Although there are no hard and fast rules, people generally lean towards Media Player when they want to listen to music, play movies and music videos, and listen to audio books, and use Media Center to view and manage media that's more complex, such as live TV, recorded TV, Internet TV, movies downloaded from services such as Netflix, and similar data.

There are many reasons for these personal preferences (since you can do many media tasks with either program), but for the most part it's slightly faster to navigate the Media Player interface, and Media Player loads significantly faster than Media Center. On a low-end netbook or laptop, it could take 2 or 3 seconds to load Windows Media Center, if not more (while Media Player loads almost instantly). If you could 'weigh' both programs, you'd say that Windows Media Player was light and agile, while Windows Media Center was heavy and a tad more cumbersome. Beyond your personal preferences, though, you will have to choose Media Center to perform certain tasks, such as watch and record live TV, view live sports programmes, watch movies using Netflix and other services, and watch Internet TV. You can't do these things in Media Player.

What you'll do

Open and explore Media Player

Play music in Media Player

Play music in Media Center

View videos in Media Player

Rip a CD

Burn a CD

Watch Internet TV

Create a slide show of pictures in Media Center

Explore other Media Center options

So, is Media Center right for you, or should you go with Media Player? If you have Windows 7 Home Basic, you won't have Media Center, so that solves one problem. There just aren't enough resources to support it, generally. If you have any other version you will have Media Center, and you should at least try it a few times. If you have a high-end laptop complete with a TV tuner, DVD player and remote control, definitely consider using it. You can move through the menus and options using the arrow keys on your keyboard or the remote, which makes Media Center a great choice if you have the resources. If you find Media Center isn't right for you, you can always go with Media Player. All versions of Windows 7 offer Windows Media Player.

If you've never used Windows Media Player, the first time you open it you'll have to work through a wizard to tell Windows Media Player how you want it to perform. You'll have two options: Express or Custom. If you're new to Media Player it's OK to select Express and accept the defaults. You can always change any options you decide you don't like after you've worked with it for a while.

After completing set-up, there's no telling what you may see. If you're connected to a home network that offers shared media, you will probably see that shared media in Media Player. If you have media on your laptop or netbook, you'll certainly see that. And if you have pictures and videos on your computer or on a shared network resource, you'll see that, too. You may even see audio books mixed in with your music files, as shown here.

Regarding the interface, you'll see familiar attributes, such as the Back and Forward buttons and menus with names you'll recognise (File, View, Tools, etc.). You'll also see tab titles – Play, Burn and Sync – on the right side of the menu bar. Look deeper and you'll see Media Guide (bottom left).

Play music in Media Player (cont.)

Opening and exploring Media Player

1. Open Windows Media Player – you can find it in the All Programs menu and on the Taskbar.

2. If you are not in the Music library, click the arrow next to the Library button and select Music, or click Music in the Navigation pane (that's the left pane).

3. In the Navigation pane, select Artist, then Album, then Genre to see the differing views. Click Music last.

4. From the Navigation Pane, select Pictures. You can also click the arrow next to the Library button to access Pictures.

5. Double-click any image. It will appear in full-screen mode and a slide show of the images in the folder will begin.

6. Position your mouse at the bottom of the screen. Notice the controls at the bottom of the slide show. You can use these controls to move through the media that's playing. Click Stop.

You access playlists, categories, folders and the like in the left pane, called the Navigation pane. You can sort your music by artist, album and genre, or you can view all music in a single list. You can customise the interface in many ways as well, and one is to right-click Music to access the command Customize Navigation Pane where you can then add categories such as year, rating, composer, and more. To play any song, simply double-click it.

10

Play music in
Media Player
(cont.)

!

Important

If Windows Media Player seems to disappear, check your Taskbar. To bring it back to the Desktop, click the Media Player icon.

Now that you're somewhat familiar with the Media Player interface, let's learn a little more about playing music. To play any music track (or view any picture, watch any video, or view other media), simply navigate to it and double-click it.

7 Click Go to Library.

8 Return to any music category.

9 Navigate to any song and double-click to play it. (This may take a few clicks, depending on the view.)

10 Use the controls at the bottom of the interface to play, pause and perform other playback tasks.

11 Continue experimenting.

12

Play music in Media Player (cont.)

Playing music in Media Player

1. Open Media Player.

2. If necessary, in the Navigation pane, click Music.

3. Click Album.

4. Double-click any album to open it and repeat with any song on the album to start playing it.

5. Click View and click Now Playing.

6. To access the controls at the bottom of the interface, position your mouse cursor there. From left to right: Shuffle (to play songs in random order), Repeat, Stop, Previous, Play/Pause, Next, Mute and a volume slider. Use these controls to manage the song and to move from one song to the next.

7. To return to the Library, click the Switch to Library button.

8. Continue experimenting with the controls until you are comfortable playing music.

Did you know?

If you can't see the menu bar, click Ctrl + M on the keyboard.

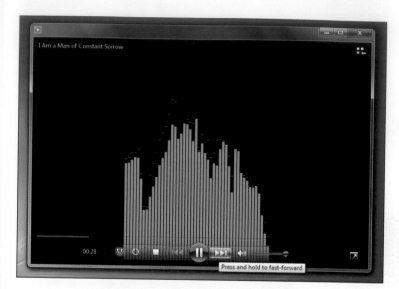

8

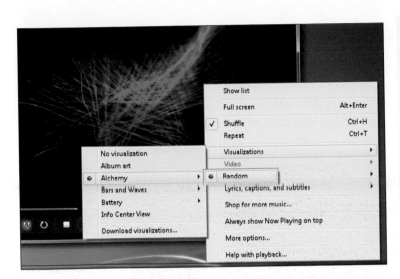

12

Did you know?

While in the Now Playing view (Step 6), right-click to choose a new 'visualisation'. A visualisation is what you see in that view. Try Alchemy, Random.

Play music in Media Center

You can also play music in Media Center. If you've never used Media Center, as with Media Player you will have to perform a few set-up tasks. Simply accept the defaults for now if prompted. Once Media Center is open (and this could take a while on a slow computer with few resources), use the arrow keys on the keyboard to navigate to the Music folder.

For your information

To see the controls in Media Center as shown here, position the mouse over the Media Center interface.

Once in the Music folder, you can browse the music in various ways. The default is Album view, but you can click artists, genres, songs, playlists, composers or years, among others, to sort the music in different ways. This is album artists view. You can also click search to look for a song, or click play all to play all the music in your library.

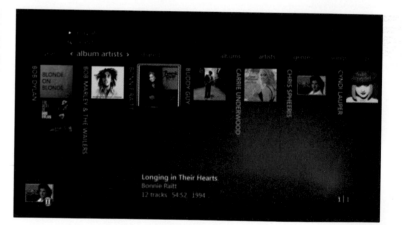

Navigating Media Center to play a specific song takes a while and there's a lot of clicking. You can simplify the task of playing a song with a right-click, though, as shown here. While you explore Media Center, right-click on various titles, icons and screens to see what's available.

Playing music in Media Center

1. Open Media Center from the Start, All Programs menu.

2. Use the arrow keys to access the Music folder.

3. Click Music Library.

4. Use the mouse or the arrow keys to locate an album, noting that other categories are available, as shown here.

5. Click once to open the album information box.

6. Click once to play any song.

12

Play music in Media Center (cont.)

7 Click play song.

8 Note the controls at the bottom of the interface. Use these to manage the media that's playing.

9 Use the Back button in the top left corner to go to a previous screen.

10 For a faster way to play an album, right-click it and click Play.

Let's head back to Media Player for a minute and see what other media can be played. Later, we'll take a similar look at Media Center. By looking at both in this manner, you can decide which program is best suited to meet your media needs.

You know you can use Media Player to locate, manage and listen to music or browse pictures, but you can do much more than that. In fact, Media Player is a great application for viewing video. This image shows some of the available video on our home network. If you look closely, you can see in the left pane that the folder being accessed is the Videos folder on a networked computer called Slimline. There are two videos shown, a music video of Michael Jackson's 'Bad', and a homemade video of a holiday to Seattle, Washington. To play a video you simply double-click it.

◀ **View other media in Media Player**

Important

If you've set up media sharing on your network, check out the available computers and libraries under Other Libraries. Navigate to them and browse what's available. You can play media from networked libraries and computers on your portable computer.

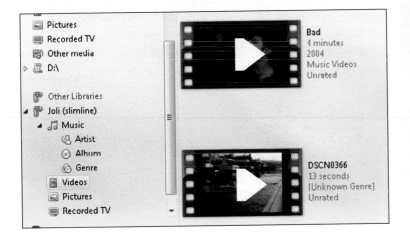

You can also view recorded TV in Media Player. You probably won't have any on a low-end laptop, but if you've dabbled in Media Center on a networked computer with a TV tuner, you may be able to access some previously recorded TV from there. Here you can see two recorded TV shows available, again from a networked PC named Slimline. The first is a recording of 'Star Trek: The Next Generation', the other is one episode of 'Modern Family'. Again, to play a video you double-click it.

View other media in Media Player (cont.)

Viewing videos in Media Player

1. Locate any video file in Media Player. You may have to look on networked computers.

2. Double-click it to play.

3. If the file is on another computer, you may have to wait while it 'buffers', or transfers to your computer.

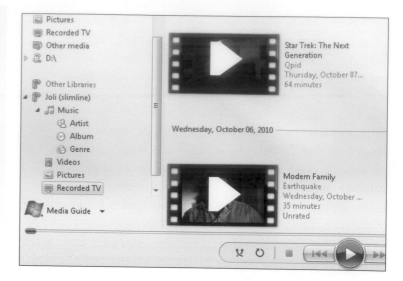

Our last example involves audio books, although we certainly haven't covered all the media you could have available to you. Audio books could be listed in any of the Music libraries, but they could also be listed in Other media. You'll have to check both areas to locate any audio books you have on your computer.

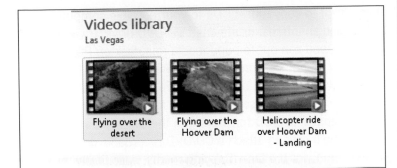

4 Alternatively, locate any video file on your computer and double-click it. By default, videos play in Media Player.

12

Rip and burn music with Media Player

Ripping a CD

1. Insert the CD to copy into the CD drive.

2. If any pop-up boxes appear, click the X to close them. This step isn't actually necessary, as you can select Rip CD in Windows Media Player from the dialogue box that appears, but I'd like to introduce ripping from Media Player, not from a dialogue box, so that you can access all available options.

3. In Media Player, deselect any songs you do not want to copy to your PC. (All songs are selected by default.)

4. In Windows Media Player, click the Rip CD button.

If you want to copy music CDs to your portable computer, you'll need an internal or attached CD/DVD drive. If you don't have one, you can opt to copy media to a desktop PC and then copy the music from that computer to your portable one over a network or via a USB flash drive. There are additional options as well. Likewise, if you want to copy music that is on your computer to a CD for playing in the car or on another CD player, you'll have to attach a CD/DVD recordable drive or use a desktop PC for the task. Copying media, specifically music, is described with two terms: rip and burn.

To rip means to copy the music on a CD to your computer's hard drive. If you have a large CD collection, this could take some time, but it will ultimately be worth it. Once music is on your computer, you can listen to it in Media Player, burn compilations of music to other CDs, and even put the music on a portable music player.

To rip a CD, simply put the CD in the CD drive, close any pop-up boxes, and in Media Player click the Rip CD button. During the copy process, you can watch the progress of the rip. By default, music will be saved in your Music folder.

For your information

Once you've ripped a CD as detailed here, you can work from the pop-up dialogue box that appears. We only want you to experience this task inside Media Player first so that you understand the interface options.

☐ ▶	1	Kinvarra's Child	2:14		Ripped to libra...
☑	2	Frank the Part Time Clo...	3:09	5	Ripping (70%)
☑	3	Mrs. Crowe's Blue Waltz	4:18		Pending
☑	4	Gebrauchmusik II	4:25		Pending
☐	5	Brooklyn Blossom	2:59		

Did you know?

You can deselect songs during the rip process if you decide you don't want to wait for them to be copied.

5 Watch as the CD is copied, you can view the rip status as shown here.

6 The ripped music will now appear in your Music library under Recently Added, as well as Artist, Album and Genre.

Burn a CD

Another way to share music is to create your own music CDs, choosing the songs to copy and placing them on the CD in the desired order. CDs you create can be played in car stereos and portable CD players, as well as on lots of other CD devices. A typical CD can hold about 80 minutes of music, but don't worry, Media Player will keep track of the songs you select and will let you know when you're running out of space on the CD you're creating.

The Burn tab in Windows Media Player can assist you in creating a CD. Burn is media-speak for copying music from your computer to a CD. Clicking Burn brings up the List pane, where Media Player will tell you to insert a blank CD if one is not in the drive already, and will allow you to drag and drop songs into the List pane to create a burn list. As music is added, the progress bar at the top of the List pane shows how much available space you've used.

For your information

Once you've added music, the Start Burn button becomes available.

Did you know?

You can right-click any song in the burn list to access additional options, including the option to delete the song from the list (not the PC), or to move up or down in the list order.

Rip and burn music with Media Player (cont.)

Burning a CD

1. Open Media Player.

2. Insert a blank, recordable CD into the CD drive and close any dialogue boxes that appear.

3. In Media Player, click the Burn tab.

4. Under Library, click Music.

5. Browse through the tracks to locate songs to add. When you find them, drag them to the List pane.

6. Drop the song in the List pane to add it to the burn list. Continue as desired.

7. Look at the slider in the List pane to verify there is room left on the CD. Continue to add songs until the CD is full or you have finished.

8. When you've added the songs you want, click Start burn.

Before we leave Media Player, it's important to note that there's quite a bit more you can do with it. One thing you may want to explore is playlists. Click the Playlists category in the left pane to see what's available. You can create your own playlists from the File menu. There are two types, a regular playlist and an auto playlist. In a regular playlist, you drag and drop songs just as you do when you create a burn list. You can then play that playlist any time you want to hear the songs on it. With an auto playlist you configure criteria. You might create a playlist for songs recently added, songs by a particular artist, or songs based on how many times you've already played them.

For your information

You do not need to fill the entire CD with songs if you don't want to.

If you have a high-end laptop – and we're talking about a really expensive, all-inclusive computer that offers just about everything you could ever want or even imagine – you can probably watch live TV on it. If that's the case, you can also record live TV, stop, pause, rewind and then fast-forward live TV, and build up a really nice digital library of TV shows. Chances are that's not what you have, though, so we're not going to talk about how to perform those tasks in this book. However, there's a good chance you have Media Center (available on Windows 7 Home Premium and higher) and an Internet connection, which means you can watch Internet TV. To get started, open Media Center and navigate to TV, internet tv.

Click internet tv once and follow the directions for getting started. Here's an example of what you might see. Click Install and follow the prompts. Once you've worked through the installation process, you'll be ready to explore Internet TV.

Watch Internet TV using Windows Media Center (cont.)

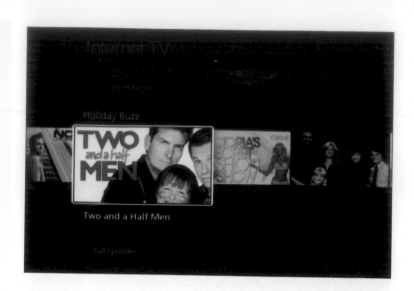

Watching Internet TV

1. In Media Center, browse to TV.

2. Click internet tv.

3. If prompted to install it or an upgrade, do so.

4. Use the arrow keys to browse through the programmes. If you find one you like, click it. Then:

   a. If applicable, choose an episode.

   b. Click play.

5. As the media plays, note the controls at the bottom of the interface. Move your mouse there to access them.

Did you know?

If you get poor performance when watching Internet TV, if possible, access a better connection, perhaps by connecting to a router with an Ethernet cable or moving closer to a wireless access point. You may get a better picture if you lessen the size of the Media Center window, too.

Another really nice thing you can do with Media Center is to play a slide show of your pictures. Just navigate to Pictures + Videos and choose picture library. You'll see your picture folders as well as the option slide shows at the top of the page. This is where you'll create your slide shows.

Unlike other slide show features you may be used to, you can hand-pick pictures from various folders on your hard drive. You aren't relegated to items in a single folder and you don't have to move any pictures around before creating the show. You simply browse folders that contain pictures, select each one to add individually, and continue adding until you've created the show you want.

Creating a slide show of pictures in Media Center

12

1 In Media Center, navigate to Pictures + Videos.

2 Click picture library.

3 Click slide show.

4 Click Create Slide Show.

5 Enter a name for the slide show and click Next.

6 Select the location to browse for media. This is most likely the picture library. Click Next.

7 Select any folder, and select each picture you want to include.

View a slide show of pictures in Media Center (cont.)

8 Click Next and if you wish, click Add More. Otherwise, click Create.

9 Repeat this process until you have added all of the desired pictures.

10 Once you've clicked Create, the slide show will appear under slide shows in Media Center.

11 Click it to play it.

12 Click play slide show.

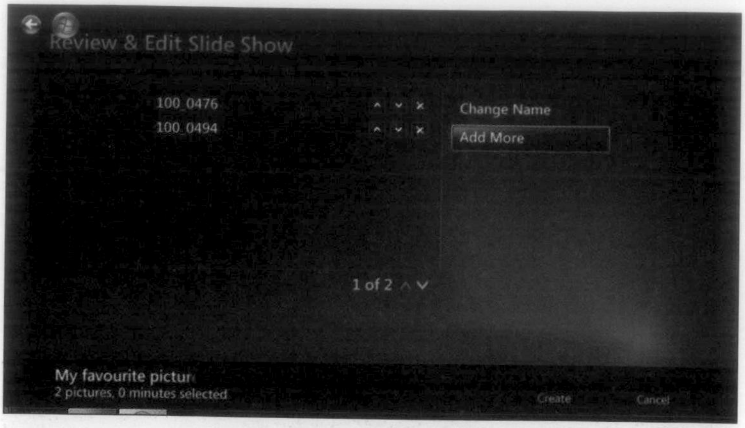

Review & Edit Slide Show

100_0476
100_0494

Change Name
Add More

1 of 2

My favourite pictur
2 pictures, 0 minutes selected

Create   Cancel

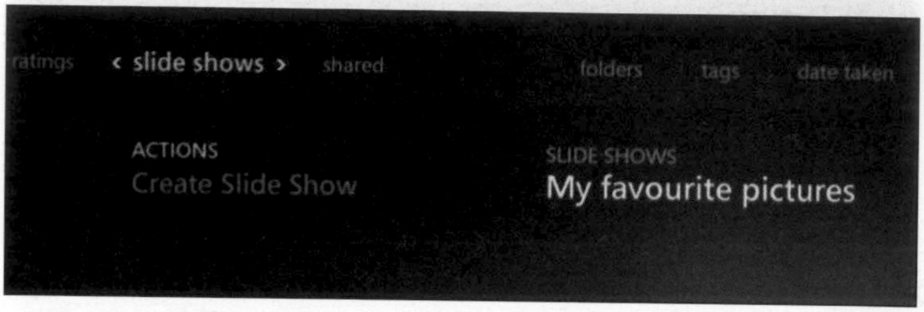

ratings   < slide shows >   shared   folders   tags   date taken

ACTIONS
Create Slide Show

SLIDE SHOWS
My favourite pictures

If you've enjoyed what you've seen so far with regard to Media Center and you want to continue using it, there are lots of other areas to explore. However, if you've decided that Media Center runs too slowly on your portable computer, you don't have the required hardware to run the program the way you'd like, or it just bogs down your media experience, there's no need to explore further.

SLIDE SHOW SCREEN SAVER

Save

Cancel

Windows Media Center can play a slide show of your favorite pictures as a screen saver.

☑ Play my favorite pictures as a screen saver

Start screen saver after

7 minutes

◀ Explore other Media Center options

Exploring other Media Center options

12

- In Pictures + Videos, click video library. You can view videos on your computer here.

- In Music, click Radio. Depending on various factors, you may be able to listen to radio stations here.

- In Movies, click play DVD to play a DVD in your DVD drive.

- In TV, click live TV. If applicable, set up your TV tuner. You can then watch live TV on your computer.

- In Sports, click on now. If you have the proper hardware, you may be able to access various sports shows that are on now.

- In Tasks, click settings. Browse through the available settings to personalise Media Center. You'll find several interesting items there, such as the ability to use your favourite pictures as a screensaver. (You'll have to designate which pictures are your favourites.)

- In Tasks, click settings and browse to Media Libraries. There you can select folders to include in your libraries.

Install and manage hardware

Introduction

You probably won't install too much external hardware on your netbook or laptop, but you may want to install a printer you use at home or a digital camera you keep with you on the road. There's more to hardware than just what you can connect, though, hence the title 'Install and *manage* hardware'. For instance, you may have problems with a specific device, either internal or external, and need to update the device driver to resolve the problem. You may want to reconfigure a power plan or create your own to get more battery life when running on stored power or to get better performance when you're plugged in. And you may want to incorporate Ready Boost, an option for enhancing your computer's performance with a USB flash drive or media card. Finally, you'll want to know where you can go to manage all hardware devices when you need to, and how to access the devices' properties pages and configuration options. You'll learn all of that and more here.

What you'll do

Install a connected printer

Install a network printer

Install a digital camera

Find and install a device driver

Update a device driver

Use Device Driver Rollback

Use Ready Boost to increase performance

Apply Sleep and Hibernate settings

Edit a power plan

Manage connected devices

! Important

On occasion, hardware manufacturers will state you need to install software first, then plug in the device, then turn on the hardware, so read the instructions that came with your hardware to know what order to do what, just as a precaution. Often, though, this is just a ruse to get you to install unnecessary software, so be aware of what you're installing.

Install a printer

Most of the time, adding hardware such as a printer you can physically connect to is a simple affair. You generally need to simply plug in the new hardware and turn it on; Windows 7 can almost always install the hardware without further intervention.

The process of installing the hardware requires a compatible driver, and for the most part, those drivers are easy for Windows to locate. There will be rare occasions when Windows 7 can't find a driver in its own driver database on the hard drive, and in these instances it will connect to the Internet and look for the driver in Microsoft's online driver database – 95–98 per cent of the time, depending on whom you ask, it is successful using one of these two methods. For the most part, speakers, headphones, printers, scanners and digital cameras all install this way.

Installing a connected printer

1 Connect the printer to a wall outlet.

2 Connect the printer to the computer using a USB cable.

3 If a pop-up message appears, click the X to close the window.

4 Turn on the device.

5 Wait while the driver is installed.

6 You can view the printer by clicking Start and then Devices and Printers.

You may want to use a printer on your network, though, and do not want to (or perhaps aren't able to) physically connect to it. In this instance you still need to install the printer, but the process is a bit different. Briefly, you open a program that offers a print command, click the Print option in a program that offers it, and in the first Print dialogue box you encounter, find and then install the desired network printer. Again, a driver must be acquired and installed for this to work successfully. In both instances, once the printer is installed, no further information is generally required and the printer will not need to be installed the next time you access it.

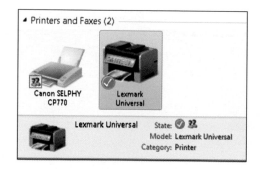

Installing a network printer

1. Open any program that offers the option to print. If you aren't sure, open WordPad.

2. Click the arrow beside the Menu button and click Print, click File and click Print, or choose another appropriate option to access a Print command.

3. In the Print dialogue box, if you don't already see the network printer, click Find Printer. Alternatively, you can click Add Printer (not shown).

13

Install a printer (cont.)

4 Browse to the printer to add and double-click it.

5 The printer will be available in the Print dialogue box after installation completes.

If you discover that some of your printer features aren't available to you, perhaps printing a mirror image, printing two-sided handouts, or increasing or decreasing the amount of ink you want to use, you may need to install the printer software that came with the printer, generally supplied on a CD or DVD. If that's the case, refer to Chapter 14 to learn how.

As noted in the previous section, we think it's best to connect new hardware, turn it on and let Windows 7 install it. Even if hardware such as printers, scanners, music players and cameras ship with additional software on a CD, you probably don't need it. Windows 7 can install just about anything, and seven times out of ten (or thereabouts), what you get on a CD is not required software anyway. You can use Windows Live Photo Gallery to import, sort and manage photos, for instance, and you can use Windows Media Player to sync devices and manage music. There will be times, of course, when you *do* need to install software from a CD. However, wait until that time arrives before you go to the trouble of installing it. And remember, on a low-end netbook at least, you should try to keep unwanted software off of your computer anyway, to reserve computer resources for more important things!

Install a digital camera

Installing a digital camera

1. Read the directions that came with the camera. If there are specific instructions for installing the driver, follow them. If not, continue here.

2. Connect the camera to a wall outlet or insert fresh batteries, and connect the camera to the computer using either a USB cable or a FireWire cable.

13

See also

If it turns out that the only way to install a particular device is to install it from a CD, refer to Chapter 14 to review your options.

Jargon buster

Driver – software that allows the PC and the new hardware to communicate with each other.

Software – a program that may not be required for the hardware to function correctly.

USB – a technology used to connect hardware to a computer. A USB cable is often used to connect a digital camera to the computer.

FireWire – a technology used to connect hardware to a computer. A FireWire cable is often used to connect a digital video camera to the computer.

Install a digital camera (cont.)

3 Turn on the camera. Place it in Playback mode if that exists. Often, simply turning on the camera is enough.

4 Wait while the driver is installed.

5 You'll see the camera in the Computer window (click Start, click Computer), shown here, and also in Devices and Printers (available from the Start menu) (not shown).

Did you know?

Devices that have their own storage areas, such as digital cameras and memory cards, often appear in the Computer window because Windows 7 sees them as external hard drives.

Sometimes a driver just can't be found or a driver that is installed is old or outdated. In this case you'll have to go looking for a compatible driver yourself, see whether an update is available for the driver you already have, or go to other lengths to make a device work. Let's start by locating a driver on the Internet, presumably for a device that failed installation when first connected.

Locate and find a driver on the Internet

As noted, almost all the time hardware installs automatically and with no input from you (other than plugging it in and turning it on). However, in rare cases, the hardware does not install properly or is simply not available. If this happens, you'll be informed that the hardware did not install and may not work properly. If you cannot replace the device with something Windows 7 recognises, you'll have to locate and install the driver yourself.

For your information

To find the manufacturer's website, try putting a www. before the company name and a .com after. (*www. epson.com*, *www.hewlett-packard.com* and *www.apple. com* are examples.)

Software Download Centre
Download drivers, software, and firmware updates for your product.

---

35. ScanGear CS (7.0.3.1a) ▶
This is a software that allows your computer to communicate with the scanner

---

◀ **Troubleshoot drivers**

Finding and installing a device driver

1 Write down the name and model number of the device.

2 Open Internet Explorer and locate the manufacturer's website.

3 Locate a link for Support, Support and Drivers, Customer Support, or something similar. Click it.

4 Locate your device driver by make, model or other characteristics. The driver may also be referred to as software, as shown here.

13

Troubleshoot drivers (cont.)

5 Click Download Driver, Obtain Software, or something similar.

6 Click Run.

7 Click Run, Install or Open Window to begin the installation.

8 Follow the directions in the set-up process to complete the installation.

Important

Install software only from manufacturers' websites – don't install drivers from third-party websites. In a worst-case scenario, it's better to replace an old or incompatible device with a new one rather than messing up your entire computer by installing corrupt or buggy software, or worse, software laden with adware or spyware.

If you already have a driver installed but the device is not performing properly, you can try to update that device driver to obtain a newer and better performing one. Updating a driver almost always resolves issues with a hardware device. You don't want to update a driver unless you can find one that's been thoroughly tested, though, because you don't want to trade one problem for another, or install a driver that's worse than the one you already have. Thus, to update a driver you should go through the Windows 7 interface that offers this option and forgo going it alone. Windows 7 will update a driver only if it has been thoroughly tested and approved. If it can't find one, it won't offer an updating option.

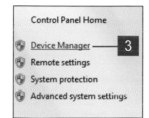

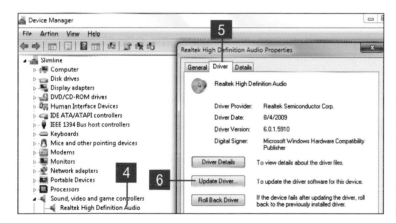

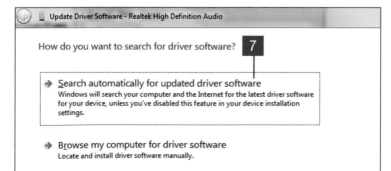

Update a device driver

Updating an existing device driver

1 Click Start and right-click Computer.

2 Click Properties.

3 Click Device Manager.

4 Expand the applicable trees and double-click the problematic device.

5 Double-click the device name and then click the Driver tab.

6 Click Update Driver.

7 Click Search automatically for updated driver software. (You must be connected to the Internet.)

8 If updated driver software can be found, it will be installed.

13

Use Device Driver Rollback

▶

Sometimes when you go looking for a driver, you create more problems than you already have. It certainly is possible to install an incompatible driver that causes the system to become unstable, for instance, or causes the device to stop working completely. Installing an incorrect driver for a device doesn't just affect the hardware you're installing, either; a bad device driver can affect your entire system. If you suspect a newly installed driver has caused a system problem or that it's worse than the one you had previously, you can roll back the new driver to the one before it using Device Driver RollBack. You can access the Roll Back Driver command in Device Manager.

Using Device Driver Rollback

1 As detailed earlier, open Device Manager.

2 Expand the applicable trees and double-click the problematic device.

3 Click the Driver tab.

4 Click Roll Back Driver. (This option will be greyed out if no new driver has been installed.)

3

Realtek High Definition Audio Properties   x

| General | Driver | Details |

Realtek High Definition Audio

Driver Provider: Realtek Semiconductor Corp.
Driver Date: 8/4/2009
Driver Version: 6.0.1.5910
Digital Signer: Microsoft Windows Hardware Compatibility Publisher

Driver Details   To view details about the driver files.

Update Driver...   To update the driver software for this device.

4 Roll Back Driver   If the device fails after updating the driver, roll back to the previously installed driver.

Disable   Disables the selected device.

Uninstall   To uninstall the driver (Advanced).

Close   Cancel

In order to understand how Ready Boost works, you have to know a little about RAM, hard drives and paging files. Let's start with RAM.

RAM, or random access memory, holds temporary data the computer needs to function. This data can be computer code, data you want to send to a printer, software commands, calculations made while rendering edits you've just made to a photo, and other temporary data. Generally, the more RAM you have, the better your computer performs. RAM comes in the form of RAM sticks, which are inserted onto the motherboard of your computer, inside the computer case. People often add more RAM to improve computer performance.

The hard drive is something else entirely. The hard drive is most often used to store data for the long term, such as documents, pictures and music, and is used to hold temporary data only when RAM is full. There's a small area of the hard drive that is reserved for data that needs to be swapped from RAM to the hard drive, called the paging file. When data has to be swapped out in this manner, performance degrades because it takes much longer to access data from a spinning drive than it does from RAM.

Since data stored in RAM can be accessed more quickly than data on a hard disk, it's best to have as much RAM as possible. On a laptop or netbook, though, adding RAM can be difficult, if not impossible, and involves opening the back of the case, a dangerous endeavour.

If you want to improve performance but don't want to add RAM, you can incorporate Ready Boost. Ready Boost lets you install a USB flash drive, memory card or other compatible device to be used as an additional paging file, which is like adding more RAM (but technically isn't). With Ready Boost, data that needs to be swapped out of RAM will be swapped to the Ready Boost media instead of the hard disk, which can then be accessed faster than data on the hard drive. The result is a noticeable increase in performance.

Use Ready Boost to increase performance

13

Jargon buster

Ready Boost is a technology that lets you improve the performance of your computer easily using a compatible external USB flash drive or media card.

Use Ready Boost to increase performance (cont.)

Using Ready Boost to increase performance

1 Insert a USB flash drive, thumb drive, portable music player or memory card into an available slot on the outside of your laptop or netbook.

2 If prompted to use the flash drive or memory card to improve system performance, click Speed up my system.

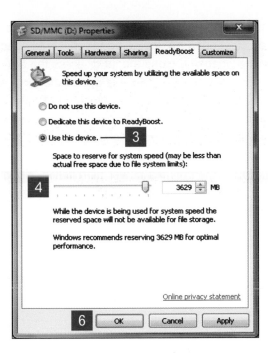

3 If the device is deemed suitable, click Use this device.

4 Define how much of the device's memory to use for performance and how much to use for file storage. Move the slider all the way to the right if you do not need to use the device for storage.

5 Leave the device plugged in.

6 Click OK.

13

Manage power options ▶

Your mobile computer comes with some very specific power options you can configure, including the ability to specify what happens when you close the lid or press the Start button. It also comes with power options in the form of three power plans: Balanced, High performance and Power saver. You can switch plans easily, to lengthen battery life (Power saver) or to get all the resources you can to play a game (High performance). You can also edit these plans or create your own. You might create a power plan called 'airplane', for instance, that, while based on the power saver settings, is edited slightly to meet your specific needs while on a plane.

It's not good for any computer to be turned 'all the way' off and then 'all the way' on too often. At least that's what many people believe, including us. Although a point of contention among experts, the facts seem to show that minimising the number of times you boot the computer will lengthen the life of the CPU, the CPU fan and the hard drive, as well as other internal components. However, when you leave a computer on all the time, it uses electricity and may create excess heat. This in turn may raise your electricity bill and/or cause heat-related problems for the laptop or netbook. To find a happy medium, then, we suggest you learn how to use hibernation and sleep settings.

You can configure what happens when you press the Start button and can tell your computer you want it to sleep when you do, but with a laptop it's much more convenient to put the computer to sleep (or into hibernation) by closing the lid. You can configure what happens when you close the lid, when you press the power button, or even when you press an available Sleep button on your laptop, from System Settings. You can also configure preferences for each of these based on whether or not your laptop is currently plugged into an electrical outlet.

Manage Sleep and Hibernate options

13

Control Panel ▸ Hardware and Sound ▸ Power Options ▸ System Settings

Define power buttons and turn on password protection

Choose the power settings that you want for your computer. The changes you make to the settings on this page apply to all of your power plans.

Power and sleep buttons and lid settings

	On battery	Plugged in
When I press the power button:	Sleep	Shut down
When I press the sleep button:	Sleep	Sleep
When I close the lid:	Shut down	Do nothing

Manage Sleep and Hibernate options (cont.)

Applying Sleep and Hibernate settings

1 Click Start and in the Start Search window type Power.

2 In the results, click Change what the power buttons do.

Before you start changing the settings, though, make sure you understand the difference between sleeping and hibernating:

- Hibernate – in this mode, the laptop will save any data that is currently saved to RAM and turn itself off. It will not draw any electricity when it's off. When you wake the laptop from hibernation, you continue where you left off, including having immediate access to open programs and files. Recovering from hibernation takes more time than recovering from Sleep mode. I suggest using Hibernate when you aren't sure when you'll use your laptop again and Sleep when you will use it very soon.

- Sleep – in this mode the computer seems as though it's turned off, but power is still provided to keep the computer's memory powered. This means what's currently in RAM stays in RAM. Sleep is a good choice when you leave your computer for lunch periods or tea breaks and want to save energy. Usually, moving the mouse or pressing a key on the keyboard will bring the computer quickly out of sleep. Recovering from Sleep mode takes a lot less time than recovering from Hibernate. I suggest you use Sleep when you know you'll be accessing your computer in the next 1–24 hours. (Note, since Sleep uses some power, if you do not have access to an electrical outlet, use Hibernate.)

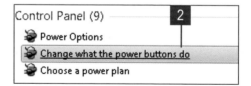

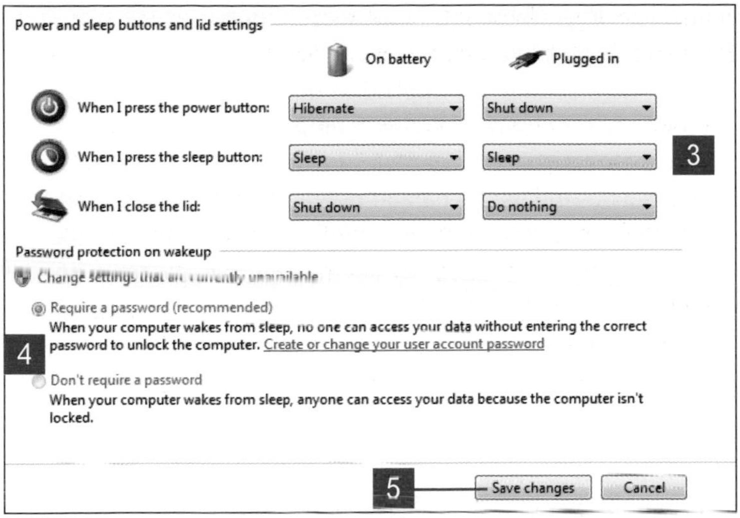

Power and sleep buttons and lid settings

	On battery	Plugged in
When I press the power button:	Hibernate ▼	Shut down ▼
When I press the sleep button:	Sleep ▼	Sleep ▼	3
When I close the lid:	Shut down ▼	Do nothing ▼

Password protection on wakeup

Change settings that are currently unavailable

⦿ Require a password (recommended)
When your computer wakes from sleep, no one can access your data without entering the correct
password to unlock the computer. Create or change your user account password

○ Don't require a password
When your computer wakes from sleep, anyone can access your data because the computer isn't
locked.

4

5 — Save changes   Cancel

3 Using the drop-down lists, make the proper choices.

4 Notice that you can require a password when the computer is awakened. It will be greyed out as shown here if you've already done that.

5 Click Save changes.

13

Edit a power plan

▶

As noted earlier, there are three preconfigured power plans: Balanced, High performance and Power saver. These are detailed here as they are applied to our Windows 7 Home Premium computer on a low-end netbook:

- Balanced – this is the default power plan. You won't get the best power savings with this plan, and you won't get the best performance either. While the laptop is plugged into a power source, the display and hard disk are turned off after 10 minutes of inactivity, and after 30 minutes the computer will go to sleep. When the laptop is running on battery power, Windows will turn off the display after 5 minutes and will sleep after 15 minutes of inactivity.

- Power saver – this plan is all about lengthening battery life. That means in all instances, even when the laptop is plugged in, you'll notice decreased brightness and processor levels, and the computer will go to sleep, turn off hard disks and turn off the display within minutes of inactivity.

- High performance – this plan is all about enhancing performance. This power plan doesn't worry about battery life. Here, Windows 7 provides 100 per cent of your CPU's processing power, which is necessary for playing games and performing resource-intensive tasks. The computer will still turn off its display, put the hard drive to sleep and put the computer to sleep after a set amount of idle time. While running on battery power, the display and sleep numbers are 10 minutes and never, respectively; when plugged in, 15 minutes and never.

You can choose any of these plans from the Taskbar's Notification area, as shown here. This enables you to quickly change any current power plan for better performance or for lengthening battery life. Alternatively, you can switch plans from the Mobility Center.

You can edit the plans from the Power Options window. You have the option of editing any of the three default plans or creating your own. Notice the option in the left pane to Create a power plan. That's what you'll choose to create your own plan, give it a name and configure your own settings. In the sidebar here, we'll cover only editing an existing plan.

Editing a power plan

1 Click Start and in the Start Search window type Power.

2 In the results, under Programs, click Power Options.

3 Click Change plan settings next to the plan you'd like to change.

4 Use the drop-down lists to make changes as desired, then click Save changes.

13

Manage connected devices

You know a little about the Devices and Printers window already, and you've learned enough about Device Manager to update and roll back device drivers. You also know that you can often see hardware in the Computer window, if that hardware looks like an external drive to Windows 7. Of all of these places, the Devices and Printers window is the best place to manage connected hardware, as it enables you to access the device, its Properties page and other options.

You open the Devices and Printers window from the Start menu. Once open, you can click any device once to see more information about it. Here, a printer has been selected. At the bottom of the page you can see the model, state and more.

You can also double-click a device. When you do that you can see various things, depending on the device itself. In our case with a network printer, we can see that the printer is ready, that no documents are in the queue, and we can even adjust print options or customise the printer. (In this view, click the Back button to return to the default Devices and Printers window.)

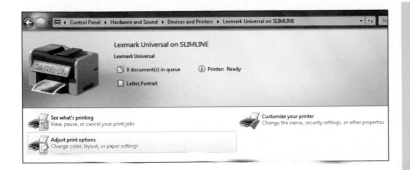

Finally, you can right-click a device and click Properties (among other things). To round out our printer example, note the options when we right-click. We can view printer properties, sure, but we can also set the printer as the default printer, set preferences, view and change properties, create a shortcut, even troubleshoot or remove the device from our computer. You'll have similar options on your own computer.

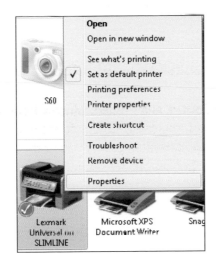

Managing connected devices

1. Click Start and click Devices and Printers.

2. Single-click any device and read the information offered in the bottom area of the screen.

3. Double-click any device. Read the information available in the resulting window.

4. Click the Back button.

5. Right-click any device and review the options.

6. Select any option to explore more.

13

Install software

14

Introduction

You will need to install software on your laptop or netbook. There are lots of ways to do this, including downloading the software from the Internet, installing from an attached or internal CD/DVD drive, installing from a shared network location, installing from a shared physical network drive including CD/DVD players and, in some instances, installing from a USB flash drive.

If this all sounds like too many choices, don't fret. You'll choose the option that is the easiest and safest for you. This means if you own a laptop that includes a CD/DVD drive and you have an installation CD/DVD, by all means use it. If you can download an application from a manufacturer's website and feel comfortable obtaining software in this manner, certainly choose that option over the others – it's often very simple. Problems arise when you own a netbook with no CD/DVD drive and really need to install software from a disk. Issues also arise when the installation files are stored on another computer and must be accessed from there for installation. In these instances, you'll have to dig a little deeper for a solution. It may be necessary to share a network drive, place the installation files on a USB flash drive or look for an alternative solution.

What you'll do

Install a program from the Internet

Connect and use a plug-and-play hard drive

Share a network drive

Copy installation files to a USB drive

?

Did you know?

There are reasons why netbooks don't come with CD/DVD drives besides minimising the thickness of the device. They can make the netbook weigh more, for one, and drain the battery while in use really quickly, for another.

One method we won't focus on here is installing software from a CD or DVD, or working through an actual installation process. We're sure you've done that and already know how. If you want to install a program from a CD or DVD and you have a drive, just insert the disk and begin the installation. The only thing we'll warn against is this: when installing software that came with hardware, make sure you're not installing anything you don't need. For instance, while you do need a digital camera driver, you probably don't need the photo-management software that comes with it. Alternatively, although a printer driver may install automatically without the CD/DVD, you may need to install the printer software so that you can access the advanced printer properties (such as printing a mirror image and managing ink consumption).

As noted in the introduction, there are lots of ways to install software. It's important to know your options so that you can choose the best method for your situation. Once you've decided on an option, it's OK to skip ahead to the appropriate part of the chapter to learn how to perform the task.

Here are several possibilities you can consider for installing software, but note that not all options will be available to you in all situations:

- Download software from the Internet – if the program you want to install is available from the Internet, and if the software can be downloaded from a trusted manufacturer's website, this is a good option for both netbooks and laptops. This is how you'll obtain most of your anti-virus software, web browsers and download-only programs such as Windows Live Essentials. The downside is not having a physical copy of the software should you need to reinstall (but you can simply download it again if you need it). If you really want a physical copy, you can sometimes copy the installation files to a CD or DVD.

- Use an external CD/DVD drive – if your netbook didn't come with a CD/DVD drive and you really need to install software from a physical disk, you can buy or borrow an external CD/DVD drive. Make sure to find one that offers a connection through a USB cable and is plug and play for easy installation.

- Share a network CD/DVD drive – you can share any networked computer's CD/DVD drive. You can then access that drive from the netbook or laptop to install a program that's stored on a CD or DVD. You'll see the familiar sharing icon once you've shared the drive successfully.

- Copy the installation files to a USB flash drive – sometimes it's possible to copy installation files to a USB flash drive and install a program from it; sometimes you can't. However, in many instances, this will work if you have no other option.

Explore installation options

Did you know?

The reason you can download a program from the Internet multiple times is because a program is generally enabled through a product key that you purchase. A downloaded program can't be used until it's activated. Free applications can also be downloaded at no risk to the publisher and no product key is required.

14

Install a program from the Internet ▶

You already know how to download and install software from the Internet – that's how you obtained Windows Live Essentials in Chapter 8. You can perform the same steps to obtain other software, too. When you opt for this solution, you don't need a CD/DVD drive and you don't even need to save the installation files to your computer. When prompted, you can simply choose to 'run' the installation routine (unless you plan to back up the installation files later, in which case you'd have to save them).

You have to make sure you obtain software from trusted publishers, though. It's never a good idea to get software from unknown websites or entities that didn't actually create the software. For instance, if you're going to install anti-virus software from the Internet, make sure you get it from a reputable site, such as Symantec or McAfee. Additionally, 'free' software rarely is. It may come with adware or spyware, or worse, or it may actually be legitimate and simply prompt you daily to purchase the full version.

When you're ready to install, follow the directions on the website. There's almost always a wizard that starts once you've clicked the appropriate number of buttons. You'll often have to click Download a few times, then Run, and then work through the installation wizard, generally accepting the defaults.

Installing a program from the Internet

1 Locate the software to download from a trusted website.

2 Read reviews if applicable and verify before starting the download that you are still on the manufacturer's website.

3 Verify you are getting the version you want and that it is compatible with Windows 7.

4 Look for Download, Download Now or a similar option.

5 Click Run to run the installation program, or click Save to save the files first and then run the program.

6 Click Run again as applicable.

7 Work through the installation wizard.

"Proven antivirus protection for free? That's what I need."

Get high-quality, hassle-free antivirus protection for your home or small business PC now.

? **Help and Support**
Help and how-to guides

Installation Video
See just how easy it is

Download Now ⬇

If you have a laptop with a CD/DVD drive and you have an installation CD/DVD, to install the program you simply insert the disk and follow the installation prompts. That's simple. If you don't have an internal drive, though, but you can buy or borrow an external one, that will do just as well. The only additional step is installation; installing a program from a CD/DVD using an external drive is the same as installing using an internal one.

Install and use a CD/DVD drive

Connecting and using plug-and-play hard drive

1 Plug the drive into an electrical outlet.

2 Connect the drive to the netbook or laptop using its USB cable.

3 Wait while the drive installs.

4 Insert the installation disk into the drive.

5 If you aren't prompted to install the disk:

   a. Click Start and click Computer.

   b. Double-click the DVD player.

   c. If you still aren't prompted, locate and open the installation file.

6 Work through the prompts to install the software.

14

Share a network drive

One of our favourite ways to install a program stored on a CD or DVD is to connect our netbook to our home network and install the CD using a shared network CD/DVD drive. You can use a wired or wireless network. The only thing you have to do is share the drive you want to use.

Sharing a network drive

1 Click Start and click Computer.

2 Right-click the CD/DVD drive and click Share with.

3 Click Advanced sharing.

4 Click Advanced Sharing.

5 Tick Share this folder and type a folder name. Click OK.

6 Click OK.

Devices with Removable Storage (1)

DVD RW Drive (E:)

Open
Open in new window
Scan with Microsoft Security Essentials...
Share with   2
Burn to disc
Shared Folder Synchronization

Advanced sharing...   3

Advanced Sharing
Set custom permissions, create multiple shares, and set other advanced sharing options.

Advanced Sharing...   4

Advanced Sharing

☑ Share this folder   5

Settings

Share name:

DVD Drive on Slimline PC

Add   Remove

Limit the number of simultaneous users to: 20

Comments:

Permissions   Caching

OK   Cancel   Apply

All that's left to do is to access that drive from your netbook or laptop. To do this, you have to be connected to the network and have applicable permissions to access the resource. One way to access the shared drive is through the Network window, although there are other ways. Once you have access, locate the installation icon to begin.

For your information

If you get a message stating you may not have permission to access the CD/DVD drive, first verify there's a CD/DVD in it. If this doesn't resolve the problem, make sure you can access other resources on the computer where the drive resides. You may need to be given specific permissions from the administrator of that computer to access the resources on it. See Chapter 6 for more information about sharing.

14

Copy installation files to a USB drive

Sometimes it's possible to copy the entire installation CD/DVD to a flash drive and then use that flash drive to install the program on your laptop or netbook. Sometimes this doesn't work (although we won't go into why). When you copy the files from a CD/DVD to a flash drive, make sure you copy all the files on the disk, as shown here.

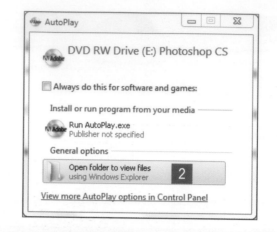

Copying installation files to a USB drive

1. Place the CD/DVD in the CD/DVD drive on any PC with a drive.

2. When prompted, click Open folder to view files. (If you aren't prompted, right-click the drive in Computer and click Open.)

3. Connect the USB flash drive. When prompted, click Open folder to view files.

4. Create a folder on the USB flash drive to hold the files. (Click New folder.)

5. Position the two windows – the CD/DVD window and the flash drive window – side by side.

6. From the CD/DVD drive window, click Edit and Select All.

7. Drag the files to the flash drive window.

Once you've copied the files to the USB flash drive, remove the drive and insert it into an available USB port on the netbook or laptop. When prompted, choose Open folder to view files. Open the folder that contains the files and locate the installation program. Double-click it to start the installation.

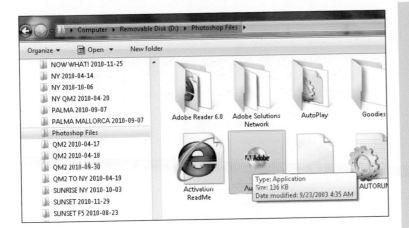

Work through the installation routine as you would with any
other installation.

Safety and security

Introduction

Windows 7 comes with a lot of built-in features to help keep you, your laptop or netbook and your data safe from Internet ills, nosy family members and coworkers, and download-happy children and spouses. Windows 7 also offers help in avoiding email and web criminals whose only purpose in life is to steal your data, get your bank account or credit card numbers, or steal your identity. Windows Live Mail (Chapter 9) even informs you if it thinks an email is 'phishing' for information you shouldn't give out. The Action Center helps too – it watches for security issues and prompts you to resolve them as they arise. Windows Update pushes out the latest security patches to your computer (provided you have it set up to do this), to help keep your computer safe.

Unfortunately, Windows 7 can't protect you all the time. This is especially true if you don't heed the warnings or don't use 'recommended' security settings, if you fail to utilise the included security tools, and if you don't install missing anti-virus/malware/adware software. It can't help you if you visit less than reputable websites either, since it's extremely hard to keep up with every Internet bad guy. And finally, Windows 7 can't help you if you let your running laptop or netbook overheat in the front seat of a hot car, leave it on the table at your local café, or drop it in a lake or swimming pool!

What you'll do

Add a new user account

More from an adminstrator to a standard account

Log in with your new, standard user account

Require a password

Configure Windows Update

Use Windows Firewall

Use Windows Defender

Resolve Action Center warnings

Use System Restore

The point we're making is this: you have to take control and be responsible for the safety and security of your laptop or netbook. It's up to you to create user accounts and passwords and to use them to log on and off your computer. It's up to you to utilise Windows Update and other system tools to your advantage. And it's up to you to heed and resolve the security warnings Windows 7 so often offers up. That's what we'll focus on here: getting secure and staying secure.

Your laptop or netbook was not shipped to you with all the available safety measures in place. While many measures are enabled by default, which you'll learn about later, some require intervention from you. Here's an example. If you let other people use your computer, they may be able to access, modify and delete your personal data, download harmful content, install applications or change settings that will affect the entire computer, all very easily. You can resolve all of these problems by creating a computer account just for them, though, something few people ever think about doing. In that same vein, every account you create should be password-protected to prevent unauthorised access, especially yours. It wouldn't do much good to create accounts and not assign passwords!

Beyond creating user accounts, here are some other ways to protect your PC, which we'll discuss in depth either in this chapter or in another:

- System Restore – if enabled, Windows 7 stores 'restore points' on your PC's hard drive. If something goes wrong you can run System Restore, choose one of these points and revert to a pre-problematic date. Since System Restore deals only with 'system data', none of your personal data will be affected (not even your last email).

- Windows Update – if enabled and configured properly, when you are online Windows 7 will check for security updates automatically and install them. You don't have to do anything, and your computer is always updated with the latest security patches and features.

- Windows Firewall – if enabled and configured properly, the firewall will help prevent hackers (people whose job it is to get into your computer and do harm to it) from accessing your computer and the data on it. The firewall blocks most programs from communicating outside the network (or outside your computer). If you want to allow a program to communicate outside your safety zone you can 'allow' a program by adding it to an 'exceptions' list. This is very easy to do.

Know what's available

Important

When you think about securing a laptop or netbook, think about all the data a thief would have access to if they stole your computer and no password was required to access the data on it.

15

Know what's available (cont.)

- Windows Defender – you don't have to do much to Windows Defender except understand that it offers protection against Internet threats. It's enabled by default and it runs in the background. However, if you ever think your computer has been attacked by an Internet threat (virus, worm, malware, etc.) you can run a manual scan here. Note that Windows Defender will be automatically disabled if you install a program that does the same thing. You need only one program running at a time; running multiple anti-virus/malware/adware programs can cause problems.

- Action Center warnings – the Action Center is a talkative application. You can be sure you'll see a pop-up if your anti-virus software is out of date (or not installed), if you don't have the proper security settings configured, or if Windows Update or the firewall are disabled. You'll learn about warnings and what to do about them in this chapter.

- Backup and Restore – this feature lets you perform backups and, in the case of a computer failure, restore them (put them back). However, there are other backup options, including copying files to a CD or DVD, copying pictures and media to an external hard drive, USB drive or memory card, or storing them on an Internet server. You'll learn about this in Chapter 16.

If every person who accesses your PC has their own standard user account and password, and if every person logs on using that account and then logs off the PC each time they've finished using it, you'll never have to worry about anyone accessing anyone else's personal data. That's because when a user logs on with their own user account, they can access only their data (and any data other users have specifically elected to share).

Additionally, every user with their own user account is provided with a 'user profile' that tells Windows 7 what desktop background to use, what screen saver, and preferences for mouse settings, sounds and more. Each user also has their own Favorites in Internet Explorer, and their own email settings, address books and personal folders. User accounts help everyone who accesses the computer keep their personal data, well, personal.

Also, by creating standard accounts for users (yes, even yourself) instead of administrator accounts, you can keep the computer safe by always requiring administrator credentials to make system-wide changes such as installing applications, changing security settings and accessing sensitive files on the computer. Even if you are the only person who accesses your laptop or netbook, you should still create a standard account for yourself and use it. If someone breaks into your home, steals your computer or accesses your computer unexpectedly, they won't be able to log on without your standard account password. If they do get logged on with your standard user account and then try to do something that may harm the computer, they'll also have to know your administrator credentials and administrator password. That being the case, hackers (or nosy family members or coworkers) won't be able to get in too easily.

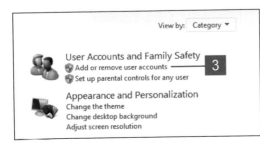

User accounts and passwords

Adding a new user account

1 Click Start.

2 Click Control Panel.

3 Click Add or remove user accounts.

4 Click Create a new account.

?

15

Did you know?

Control Panel has two views. If you don't see what's shown here, click Large icons or Small icons and click Category.

User accounts and passwords (cont.)

5 Type a new account name. This should be the user's name.

6 Verify Standard user is selected.

7 Click Create Account.

8 Click the new account.

9 Click Create a password.

10 Type the new password, type it again to confirm it and type a password hint.

11 Click Create password.

12 Click the X in the top right corner to close the window.

Important

If your administrator account is not password-protected, or if you see any other accounts that are not password-protected, work through the set of instructions to require passwords to apply them.

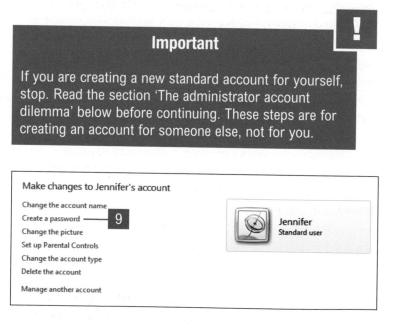

Name the account and choose an account type

This name will appear on the Welcome screen and on the Start menu.

5 Jennifer

6 ⦿ Standard user
Standard account users can use most software and change system settings that do not affect other users or the security of the computer.

○ Administrator
Administrators have complete access to the computer and can make any desired changes. Based on notification settings, administrators may be asked to provide their password or confirmation before making changes that affect other users.

We recommend that you protect every account with a strong password.

Why is a standard account recommended?

7 Create Account   Cancel

Important

If you are creating a new standard account for yourself, stop. Read the section 'The administrator account dilemma' below before continuing. These steps are for creating an account for someone else, not for you.

Make changes to Jennifer's account

Change the account name
Create a password —— 9
Change the picture
Set up Parental Controls
Change the account type
Delete the account

Manage another account

Jennifer
Standard user

?

Did you know?

You can also click Change the picture, Change the account name, Remove the password and other options to further personalise the account.

!

Important

From now on, when you've finished using the computer, either turn it off, lock it or log off of your account to protect it.

The administrator account dilemma

It's very likely you're logging onto your PC using an administrator account. That's because when you set up Windows 7, it made you create an administrator account! Nowhere did it tell you to create a standard account later, or otherwise inform you of the importance of it. Basically, if an administrator account is being used, a hacker, child, thief or other person or Internet threat (such as a virus or worm) could, theoretically at least, do more damage than if you were logged on with a standard user account. Standard users have fewer rights and privileges, and thus so would whatever threat arrived at your computer through that account.

The problem with simply creating a new standard user account for yourself is that all your data, preferences, media, Internet Explorer Favorites, contacts, email, etc. would have to be moved from your old account to the new one. This would take a long time. Thus, you don't want to just create a new standard account and start using it; the new account would look like your computer looked the first time you used it. What you want to do is create a new *administrator* account, log in with it and then downgrade your administrator account to a standard one. This will enable you to keep all your settings, data, email, contacts, Favorites, etc. intact. It'll be almost like nothing happened at all!

15

User accounts and passwords (cont.)

Moving from an administrator to a standard account

1 Click Start.

2 Click Control Panel.

3 Click Add or remove user accounts.

4 Click Create a new account.

5 Type Admin for the account name. Select Administrator.

6 Click Create Account.

7 Click the new Admin account.

8 Click Create a password.

9 Type the new password, type it again to confirm it and type a password hint.

To find out whether you're logging on using an administrator account:

1. Click Start.

2. Click Control Panel.

3. Click Add or remove user accounts.

4. If the account you log on with says Administrator, as shown here, you're using an administrator account.

Important

If you find that your administrator account is not protected by a password, click it and click Create a password.

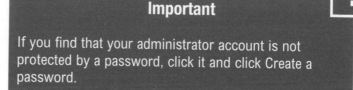

Important

When creating a password, it's best to choose one that contains upper- and lower-case letters and a few numbers. Write down the password and keep it somewhere out of sight and safe. Each time you need to make a system-wide change, you'll need to input Admin and the password to obtain access.

Make changes to Joli's account

Change the account name
Change the password
Remove the password
Change the picture
Set up Parental Controls
Change the account type ——— 13
Delete the account

Manage another account

Joli
Administrator
Password protected

Devices and Printers

Default Program

Help and Suppor

Switch user
Log off — 3
Lock

Restart

Sleep
Hibernate

Shut down ▶

10 Click Create password.

11 Click the back arrow as needed to return to the window that contains the list of user accounts.

12 Click your old administrator account, not the new Admin account.

13 In the resulting window, click Change the account type.

14 Click Standard user.

Logging in with your new, standard user account

1 Click Start.

2 Click the right arrow.

3 Click Log off.

4 Log back in using your new standard account (which is your old user name and credentials).

15

User accounts and passwords (cont.)

Requiring passwords

1 Click Start.

2 Click Control Panel.

3 Click add or remove user accounts.

4 Click the user account to apply a password to.

5 Click Create a password.

6 Type the new password, type it again to confirm it and type a password hint. It's best to create a password that contains upper- and lower-case letters and a few numbers. Write down the password and keep it somewhere out of sight and safe.

7 Click Create password.

8 Click the X in the top right of the window to close it.

Important

When logged on as a standard user, to make a change to the system that affects everyone you will either be prompted to enter the Admin password or simply be told you are not allowed to make this change. If prompted that you simply don't have access, you'll have to log off and log back on as Admin to complete the change. It's much more likely you'll be prompted to input the Admin password. What you see depends on how other security features are configured. Whatever happens, the security enhancement you get by using a standard account far outweighs the nuisance of the occasional security message.

Although Windows 7 comes with lots of system utilities, there are three that are well suited to be detailed in this chapter: Windows Update, Windows Firewall and Windows Defender. All three can help you protect your computer from Internet threats.

Windows Update

It's very important to configure Windows Update to get and install updates automatically. This is the easiest way to ensure your computer is as up to date as possible, at least for patching security flaws Microsoft uncovers, having access to the latest features and obtaining updates to the operating system itself. I propose you verify that the recommended settings are enabled as detailed here and occasionally check for optional updates manually.

When Windows Update is configured as recommended here, updates will be downloaded automatically when you are online (on the Internet), installed and, if necessary, your computer will be rebooted automatically. You can configure the time of day you want this to happen.

System and Security
Review your computer's status
Back up your computer
Find and fix problems

For your information

The Windows Help and Support Center offers pages upon pages of information regarding Windows Update, including how to select updates when more than one is available. I think the above paragraphs state all you need to know as an average laptop/netbook computer user and thus you need not worry about anything else regarding Windows Update. If at any time you are running low on disk space, opt to remove data over choosing not to install security updates.

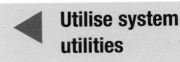

Utilise system utilities

Configuring Windows Update

1 Click Start.

2 Click Control Panel.

3 Click System and Security.

4 Click Windows Update.

15

Utilise system utilities (cont.)

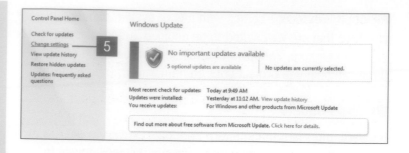

5 You may see that Windows is up to date, or you may see that there are optional or available updates. Whatever the case is, click Change settings.

6 Verify the settings are configured to Install updates automatically (recommended) as shown here.

7 Notice the default time of 3:00 a.m. Change this to a time when your PC is connected to the Internet but is not being used. This is not necessary, actually – if the computer is not online at 3:00 a.m., it will check for updates the next time it is.

8 Make changes if needed and click OK.

Did you know?

If you see that optional components are available (or any other updates for that matter), you can view and install them by clicking the blue link to the updates. Select the items to update and click OK. You do not have to install optional updates.

There are two more security features to explore: Windows Firewall and Windows Defender. There isn't much you need to do with these features except to make sure they are both enabled and are protecting your computer. By default, both are enabled.

Windows Firewall

Windows Firewall is a software program that checks the data that comes in from the Internet (or a local network) and then decides whether it's good data or bad. If it deems the data harmless, it will allow it to come through the firewall; if not, it's blocked. You need a firewall to keep hackers from getting access to your computer and to help prevent your computer from sending out malicious code if it is ever attacked by a virus or worm.

Sometimes the firewall will block programs you want to use, including but not limited to:

- Windows Live Messenger
- Microsoft Office Outlook
- Remote Assistance
- Windows Media Player
- Wireless Portable Devices.

These and others are blocked by default, and the first time you try to use them you'll be prompted to unblock them. There is reasoning behind this, and it has to do with protecting you from Internet ills. A hacker may try to come through the Internet to your PC using an application you don't normally use, such as Remote Assistance. It can't come through unless you 'allow' it to, though. (When unblocking a program you can ask that you will not be prompted again regarding that particular application.)

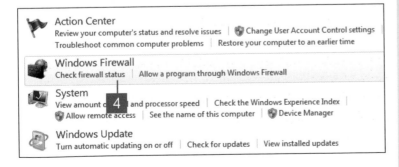

Using Windows Firewall

1 Click Start.

2 Click Control Panel.

3 Click System and Security.

4 Under Windows Firewall, click Check firewall status.

15

Utilise system utilities (cont.)

5 Verify the firewall is On. If not, select Turn Windows Firewall on or off.

6 Enable the firewall and accept the default settings. Click OK.

7 Click OK.

Important

!

If you work through the steps for using Windows Firewall and it is turned off, it may be turned off because you have a third-party firewall installed. If you aren't sure, go ahead and enable Windows Firewall. If you know you have a third-party firewall, don't enable it. Running two firewalls can cause problems for the computer.

Windows Defender

Windows Defender protects your PC against malicious and unwanted software. Generally this is a type of data called spyware, malware or adware. Spyware can install itself on your PC without your knowledge and can wreak havoc by causing these types of problems:

- adding toolbars to Internet Explorer
- changing Internet Explorer's Home page
- taking you to websites you do not want to visit
- showing pop-up advertisements
- causing the computer to perform slowly
- stealing sensitive data such as user names and passwords.

Windows Defender helps protect you from getting this type of data on your computer in the first place and thus limits infection on PCs. It's up to you to make sure that Windows Defender is running and configured properly, or that you have a substitute program running. (You are already protected if you installed Microsoft Security Essentials and thus can skip this section.) It's important to note that Windows Defender is not an anti-virus program. Windows 7 does not come with one and you have to obtain your own.

Jargon buster

Adware – Internet advertisements (which are also applications) that often include additional code that can be used to track a user's personal information and pass it on to third parties, without the user's authorisation or knowledge.

Virus – a self-replicating program that infects computers with intent to do harm. Viruses often come in the form of an attachment in an email.

Worm – a self-replicating program that infects computers with intent to do harm. However, unlike a virus, it does not need to attach itself to a running program.

Using Windows Defender

1. Click Start.

2. In the Start Search window, type Windows Defender.

3. Under the results for Control Panel, click Windows Defender.

4. If you find that Windows Defender is turned off, don't turn it on if you have another anti-malware or anti-adware program running. You only need one!

5. If Windows Defender is enabled, hopefully you'll see that no unwanted or harmful software has been detected. If not, you'll be prompted regarding what to do next. (This is highly unlikely.) Click Tools.

15

Utilise system utilities (cont.)

6 Click Options.

7 Verify that Automatic scanning is enabled.

8 If desired, change the approximate time of the scan. It's best to leave the other defaults as they are.

9 Click Save if you've made changes or Cancel if not.

10 Click the arrow next to Scan (not the Scan icon). Note that you can manually perform a Quick scan or a Full scan. Do this if you think the computer has been infected.

11 Click the X in the top right corner to close the Windows Defender window.

For your information

Check out the additional option in Windows Defender in addition to Automatic scanning. Click each option to view it.

The Action Center amasses data regarding problems your computer has encountered and searches for solutions. When solutions become available, you'll be informed. Additionally, the Action Center scans regularly to make sure that your anti-virus software is installed, that your automatic backups (if configured) are running smoothly, and that other computer components are healthy.

You need to occasionally visit the Action Center to see whether any warnings exist or there's any issue you need to resolve. If you see anything listed in red, the problem needs to be resolved immediately. You may also see items listed in yellow, which are less urgent but still important.

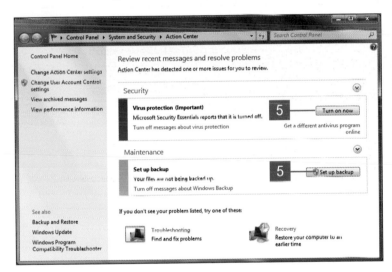

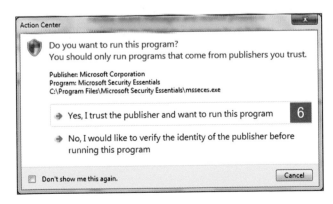

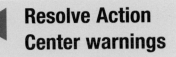

Resolve Action Center warnings

Resolving Action Center warnings

1 Click Start.

2 Click Control Panel.

3 Click System and Security.

4 Click Action Center.

5 If there's anything in red (or yellow) read about the problem. If there's an option to resolve it, click it. Here you can see an option for virus protection, Turn on now. Set up backup is also available.

6 Note the resolution and perform the task.

15

Resolve Action Center warnings (cont.)

7 Continue resolving issues as necessary. The Action Center should look like this when you've finished.

Review recent messages and resolve problems

No issues have been detected by Action Center.

7

Security ⌄

Maintenance ⌄

If you don't see your problem listed, try one of these:

Troubleshooting
Find and fix problems

Recovery
Restore your computer to an earlier time

?

Did you know?

To change how often you're notified about changes made to your computer, click User Account Control Settings in the Action Center window.

System Restore, by default, regularly creates and saves *restore points* that contain information about Registry settings and deep-down system information that Windows uses to work properly. You can use these restore points to recover from a system error, problematic installation or general computer problem. Because System Restore works only with its own system files, it can't recover a lost personal file, email or picture, though; it's just for system files and for resolving system problems. In the same vein, running System Restore will not affect this data either.

In a nutshell, then, System Restore lets you restore your computer to an earlier time without affecting any of your personal files, including documents, spreadsheets, email and photos (among other things). You can use System Restore if and when you install a program or driver that ultimately produces error messages or causes problems for the computer, and uninstalling the problematic application or driver doesn't resolve the issue.

Important

System Restore can't be enabled unless the computer has at least 300 MB of free space on the hard disk, or if the disk is smaller than 1 GB.

We rarely come across a computer where System Restore has been disabled. Thus, here we'll show you how to check for restore points and access them, and how to use System Restore if you need to.

Use System Restore

15

Use System Restore (cont.)

Using System Restore

1. Click Start.

2. In the Start Search box, type System Restore.

3. Click System Restore under the Programs results.

4. Read the information and click Next.

5. Verify that restore points are available and select a restore point. You'll want to select a point that is just prior to the problem occurring.

6. Click Next.

7. Click Finish to run System Restore, otherwise click Cancel.

System Restore

Restore system files and settings

System Restore can help fix problems that might be making your computer run slowly or stop responding.

System Restore does not affect any of your documents, pictures, or other personal data. Recently installed programs and drivers might be uninstalled. Is this process reversible?

< Back   **Next >**   Cancel

4

System Restore

Restore your computer to the state it was in before the selected event

How do I choose a restore point?

Current time zone: Central Standard Time

Date and Time	Description	Type
12/9/2010 2:25:30 PM	Windows Update	Critical Update
12/9/2010 2:18:41 PM	Windows Update	Critical Update
12/8/2010 11:03:16 AM	Windows Update	Critical Update
12/4/2010 8:54:23 PM	WLSetup	Install
12/4/2010 8:53:23 PM	Installed DirectX	Install
12/4/2010 8:52:34 PM	Installed DirectX	Install
12/4/2010 8:51:12 PM	Windows Update	Critical Update
12/4/2010 8:49:53 PM	Windows Live Essentials	Install
12/4/2010 5:10:05 PM	Installed iTunes	Install

5

☐ Show more restore points   Scan for affected programs

< Back   **Next >**   Cancel

6

Important

!

If no restore points are available or if you find that System Restore isn't running, you'll need to enable it. You can do this from the System Properties dialogue box, available by clicking Start and right-clicking Computer, then clicking Properties. Click System Protection in the left pane.

Backing up and syncing data

Introduction

To keep the data on your netbook or laptop safe, you'll need to protect your computer with a password and physically protect the computer from theft, heat, loss, rain and other dangers. You'll also need to back up the data on it regularly, partly because you may slip in your protective endeavours. Backing up is extremely important for all computers, but especially for portable ones. It's pretty easy to drop a laptop into a swimming pool or leave it on the boot of the car and drive off without it. As you can guess, these aren't real dangers with a desktop PC.

Another task that goes hand in hand with backing up a portable computer is syncing another device with one. You may want to sync a portable device such as a BlackBerry or iPhone. You may simply want to sync music you store on a music player. Additionally, you can sync a device such as an iPad for the sole purpose of backing up the data you have on your laptop. iPads and similar devices make great external backup devices, because they can be configured to sync your photos, videos, audio books, contacts, calendar information and more. Windows 7 offers its own programs for syncing, too. You can sync devices using the Devices and Printers window and Media Player, if the device is compatible and recognised by Windows.

What you'll do

Use Windows Backup and Restore

Copy data files to a USB drive

Connect a device to sync

Get iTunes

Devices and Printers

Explore backup options

There are many ways to back up your data. You can use the Windows 7 Backup and Restore program, you can drag and drop data files to an external hard drive, flash drive and/or network share, you can store data 'in the cloud' on network servers on the Internet, and you can burn data to DVDs and CDs, to name just a few. We suggest at least using a combination of two, the drag-and-drop technique coupled with the Windows Backup and Restore program. This will offer two ways to recover data if it goes missing, and if one method fails (for whatever reason), the other method can be used as a backup.

We further suggest that you supplement this technique, if possible, with some online option for saving data. You could save copies of your will, power of attorney and medical directives on a web server that you also permit your children or parents to access. In case of an emergency, the data is available. You may decide to include additional files there, too. Consider SkyDrive (Chapter 8) or Office Live Workspace (Chapter 17) for this.

Windows Backup and Restore is available from Start, All Programs and Maintenance. To use Windows Backup and Restore, however, you first need to have some place to save the restore files. This can be almost any place except a folder on the drive you're backing up (or on any partition or volume on your netbook or laptop). Backing up data on the same computer you want to protect doesn't do any good at all – if something destroys your laptop, it'll destroy that backup, too. You must save your backup somewhere outside of your computer's hard drive (and that's actually a requirement).

So, think about what you can use to store the backup and how to protect that backup once it's created. Whatever you choose needs to be something you can connect to regularly, such as a networked computer, external hard drive, or perhaps even a high-capacity USB flash drive. You can also save to CDs and DVDs, and if you have a drive on your laptop, that's another way to go. We find this option a bit inconvenient, though, since multiple CDs will be required and, possibly, multiple DVDs. Additionally, since you have to physically insert those CDs, the task can't be completely automated.

Once the backup is created, you should be able to move it to a safe place, such as a lock box of some sort, your parents' or children's house, or somewhere similar. However, as is the case with an external hard drive, you'll have to reconnect the device when a scheduled backup is about to occur. Thus, if you're using an external drive, you may want to create copies of your backup files to keep off site, while keeping the device handy.

There are a few caveats with regard to Backup and Restore. First, you can save your backups on a network location only if you're using Windows 7 Professional or Ultimate, so a network location may not be an option for you. Since most readers won't have these editions, we won't spend time covering how to do that, either. Second, wherever you choose to save your backups must be available each time you perform a backup. This means that if you schedule a backup to occur once a week using an external drive network drive or another resource, your laptop or netbook must be able to access the resource to save the backup to in order to work. The latter

Use Windows Backup and Restore

Use Windows Backup and Restore (cont.)

may cause a problem if you use an external drive and then disconnect and move the drive for safekeeping. But rest assured, if a backup does not complete for whatever reason, you'll be informed by the Action Center (seen here).

Using Windows Backup and Restore

1. Connect the backup device you want to use and connect the netbook or laptop to an electrical outlet.

2. Click Start. In the Start Search window, type Backup.

3. In the results, under Programs, click Backup and Restore.

4. Click Set up backup.

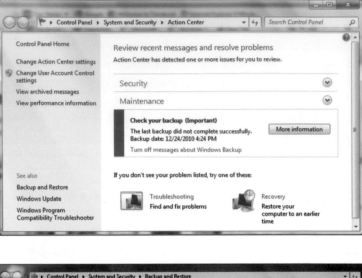

Important

Since backups can be large, consider a high-capacity USB drive, external hard drive or DVDs. You can also choose a network location if you have the proper version of Windows 7. For the first backup, if possible select a location that has lots of GB of space, such as an external hard drive, just to be safe.

Select where you want to save your backup

We recommend that you save your backup on an external hard drive. Guidelines for choosing a backup destination

Save backup on:

Backup Destination	Free Space	Total Size
Backup Drive (E:) [Recommended]	217.29 GB	465.11 GB

5

Refresh

Next   Cancel

5 When prompted, choose a place to save your backup.

For your information

To choose a network location, such as another computer on your home network, click Save on a network (if you have that option). Locate the folder and input credentials to access the computer (your administrator name and password will do). Click OK to apply the changes.

Did you know?

You can't create a backup on the hard disk of the computer you are backing up.

Use Windows Backup and Restore (cont.)

6   Click Next. (If prompted for any other information, such as a hard drive partition, to insert a blank DVD or insert a USB drive, do so.)

7   Select what to back up. First timers should select Let Windows choose (recommended). Click Next.

8   Note the time and date for the backups to occur. If you want to, click Change schedule and choose settings for how often, what day and what time future backups should occur.

9   Click Save settings and run backup.

You can watch the progress of the backup if you wish. First-time backups could take quite a bit of time, though. Click View Details if you're really interested in what's going on.

For your information

Should you ever need to restore data from a backup, connect the device where the backup is stored, start the Backup and Restore program, and opt to 'restore' files instead of back them up.

Drag and drop to an external drive ▶

Dragging and dropping your important and recently changed files to an external device once a month is a good addition to any backup strategy. Why? Because, for whatever reason, you may not be able to recover data using the Windows Backup and Restore file. For instance, if your netbook or laptop was stolen, and you decided you wanted an Apple computer instead, you would not be able to use the data you had so carefully acquired through Backup and Restore. Additionally, even the best-laid plans can go awry when a backup becomes 'corrupt' due to a virus or some other problem, goes missing with the laptop or netbook due to theft, fire or flood, or for just about any other reason imaginable. That's why it's important to have a non-proprietary and hand-picked backup of your most important data. You can also use dragging and dropping to quickly back up data you've recently changed, added or edited, when the next scheduled backup with Backup and Restore won't occur for a while. Dragging and dropping is a great way to perform daily backups.

Finally, it's easy to hide a USB drive, memory card and the like (as well as lose it, so be careful), which makes it easy to send home a copy of your latest backup with your parents or children for a bit of extra security. If it's really important, perhaps a safe deposit box or lock box is in order, too.

The best way to perform one of these kinds of backups is to set up your screen so that the USB drive takes up one half of it and the folders you wish to copy take up the other half. As an example, you could open a window for your flash drive on the left and a window for your personal folders on the right. Then all you have to do is drag and drop files between them. You learned how to do this in Chapter 14, when you copied a CD's installation files to a USB flash drive. It is the same concept here.

Copying data files to a USB drive

1 Open the folder that contains the files you want to copy.

2 Drag the window to one side of the screen so that it takes up half (it'll snap into place).

3 Connect the USB flash drive. When prompted, click Open folder to view files.

4 Create a folder on the USB flash drive to hold the files, if applicable. (Click New folder.)

5 Drag this window to the other side of the screen so that it snaps into place and takes up half of it.

6 Select the files to copy.

7 Drag the files to the flash drive window, while holding down the right-most button.

8 Let go of the mouse button and click Copy here.

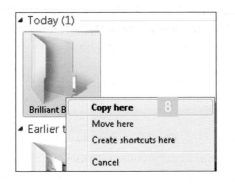

For your information

It's not technically necessary to drag and drop while holding down the right-mouse key; however, it is a good habit to get into. When dragging and dropping in this manner, you'll always be given the option to move or to copy. When you drag and drop while left-clicking, you are not prompted and specific rules are applied automatically.

Drag and drop to a network drive

The process for copying data to a network drive is just about identical to copying data to a USB flash drive, except instead of opening the USB drive window, you open a window that contains the network resource and the folder you want to use. You can open a network window from any Explorer window, including your personal folder window available from the Start menu. You'll find Network in the bottom left of that window. Browse through the network until you find the network resource. Here, we'll choose the Backup Drive on Slimline, which is a computer with shared resources enabled. Once you've found the proper folder, position the two windows side by side as detailed in the previous section and drag and drop as you wish.

You may be familiar with syncing. You may already sync an iPhone, a BlackBerry, an MP3 player, or a similar device. You know that syncing allows you to keep two devices in tune with one another by copying data between them as data changes. For instance, if you use an iPhone to create a Calendar event, when you connect and then sync that device to your laptop, the event is added to the calendar program on your laptop or netbook.

Explore sync options

16

Connecting a device to sync

1 Turn on the device if applicable.

2 Use the cable provided with the device to connect it to your laptop. Generally this is a USB cable.

3 Wait while the device is installed.

Did you know?

Technically, syncing is the process of keeping files matched, when those files are used on more than one device.

Most of the time, syncing devices with your laptop or netbook is best achieved using their specific syncing software. A BlackBerry uses BlackBerry Desktop software; iPad, iPods, etc. use Apple's iTunes software. Some devices don't have their own syncing software, though, such as generic MP3 players, pay-as-you-go mobile phones and similar devices. In these cases you may be able to use the Devices and Printers window or Windows Media Player to manage syncing tasks.

The best way to see whether there's an option for syncing built into the device or associated with it is to read the information that came with the device and then connect it. On connection you may be prompted to download and/or install specific software. You may also find that the Devices and Printers window recognises the device, offering another option for syncing.

Installing device driver software
Click here for status.
3

Backing up and syncing data 285

Explore sync options (cont.)

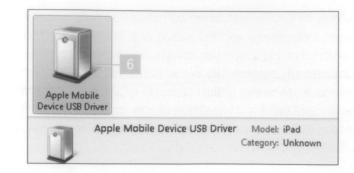

Apple Mobile Device USB Driver

| Apple Mobile Device USB Driver | Model: iPad |
| | Category: Unknown |

4 Wait to see if any information appears. You may see a prompt to install specific software, for instance.

5 If no information appears, click Start and click Devices and Printers.

6 Double-click the device to learn more about it.

Did you know?

Most devices have explicit instructions that come with them. The iPad, for instance, needs iTunes to be activated and you'll be required to install it.

You sync devices with your laptop to keep data 'matched'. If you use an MP3 player to listen to music and you obtain new songs on your netbook or laptop, you want those songs to be transferred automatically to the device when you connect it. Likewise, if you use a BlackBerry or iPhone to manage a calendar and tasks, you want those items to be synced to your laptop or netbook when you connect them. For the most part, you'll use the device's associated program.

If a program isn't required or available, you may be able to use the Devices and Printers window or Media Player to perform syncing tasks, both included with Windows 7. We'll introduce these as options here and show you how to get started, but because devices vary from one make and model to another, ultimately it will be up to you to set up the syncing process between devices.

iTunes

iTunes is a media program created by Apple for use with iPods, iPads, iPhones, etc. You need it to activate these devices, back them up and sync them with your computer. Some people like to use iTunes even if they don't have an i-device. If you didn't take to Media Player or Media Center in Chapter 12 for managing music, you may prefer iTunes.

Explore syncing software

16

Getting iTunes

1 Visit *www.apple.com/itunes*.

2 Click Download iTunes, then Download Now.

3 Work through the installation process.

4 Open iTunes and connect your compatible device.

5 Your device may begin to sync, but you can stop the sync manually if you wish.

6 Click the device in the left pane.

7 Work through the tabs to set up syncing.

8 Continue experimenting as desired.

Explore syncing software (cont.)

Exploring Devices and Printers

1 Connect your portable device.

2 Click Start and click Devices and Printers.

3 Locate and then double-click the device.

4 Review syncing options.

5 Configure syncing options as desired and as applicable for your device.

Devices and Printers

When you connect an MP3 player, it will appear in the Devices and Printers window, as shown here. Note the option to set up syncing. If you double-click Set up sync, a new window will appear, also shown. From there you can choose what to sync. What you'll see in this window depends on the device. Here, with our Sony Walkman, we can sync Music, Pictures and Videos. You may see fewer options, or perhaps additional ones, when you connect different devices.

If you opt to sync the device, you can choose exactly what to sync by selecting specific folders on your computer's hard drive. Once you've set it up, just click Sync now.

Media Player

It's likely that this same device that was recognised in Devices and Printers will be recognised in Windows Media Player. Connect the device, open Media Player and click the Sync tab to find out. As you can see here, it's possible to use Media Player to drag and drop playlists, albums, songs and other media directly to the sync list in the right pane. Once you've told Media Player what you want to sync, the Start sync button will become active.

Sync Center is a feature of Windows 7 that allows you to check the results of your recent sync activity if you've set up your computer to sync files with a network server. This allows you to access copies of your network files even when your computer isn't connected to the network. Sync Center is most often used in business scenarios where a laptop user needs to work on company files while away from the office, and is generally set up by a knowledgeable network administrator. If you'd like to see it, Sync Center is available from Start, All Programs, Accessories.

Explore syncing software (cont.)

When you first open Sync Center you won't see any 'sync partnerships'. You'll have to create these partnerships. That's because Sync Center is used to sync files with network locations, not simple devices such as MP3 players. If you want to sync with mobile phones and the like, you can use the Devices and Printers window, sometimes Media Player, and you can opt for third-party software.

Explore online storage

17

Introduction

If you have a laptop or netbook with a large hard drive, you can probably store as much data as you want to on it without having to worry about running out of hard drive space. Because of this, you may feel tempted to skip this chapter. However, storing data online offers a great way to back up data and also enables you to access the data from any computer with Internet access. Having access to your most important data from anywhere at any time (even when you don't have your laptop or netbook with you) can be extremely useful. Online storage also offers a place to securely store sensitive data you'd rather not leave on your laptop, to protect yourself if your laptop is ever lost or stolen.

If you have a small netbook with limited storage resources, storing data online is a must. This is probably the case if you've opted for a netbook that has a solid-state hard drive, because these types of drives generally hold much less data than traditional hard drives. The first solid-state drives (on netbooks anyway) offered only 4 GB to 8 GB of storage space, while traditional drives offered 160 GB or more. If your netbook holds only, say, 32 GB of data, you're going to run out of hard drive space very soon unless you incorporate online storage (or some kind of external storage).

You can share data online in various ways, and we certainly can't introduce every option here. However, there are lots of easy options for sharing, including using Facebook to make your photos and videos accessible to others. If you have always-accessible Internet, you can log on and view those media files from anywhere too. You can store videos to YouTube as well, although we won't go into that here, and you can store photos with Flickr. At Flickr you have access to editing tools and multiple ways to share your photos with others, group them and manage them online.

Finally, you may be interested in storing sensitive documents or backups to online servers you can access anywhere. For this we'll introduce SkyDrive. Finally, we'll show you how to find additional options.

Facebook is a very popular social networking site where you can input information about yourself, add friends, and post photos and videos, among other things. You can use your Facebook to share photos and video with others. Facebook is a great way to make your favourite photos and videos accessible from anywhere, share them with your friends and family and show them off on your laptop or netbook.

Important !

Generally you copy any pictures or videos to your hard drive prior to uploading them to Facebook (and then remove them afterwards). If the images are on a media card, you can try to upload them directly from the card, though, saving a step or two.

Uploading photos and video to Facebook

17

1 Create an account and log into *www.Facebook.com*.

2 To add a photo or create an album with multiple photos:

a. Click Photo.

b. Choose to upload a photo, take a photo, or create an album.

c. Click Browse or Select Photos to locate the photos to add. What you see will depend on your choice in Step 2b.

d. Work through the wizard pages to add your photos.

3 To upload a video:

a. Click Video.

b. Click Record a Video or Upload a Video.

c. Depending on your choice in the previous step, either record or browse to the video to upload.

d. Complete any remaining steps.

Store photos with Facebook and Flickr (cont.)

Flickr is another social networking-type website where you can upload, store and share photos easily. This keeps the photos off of your hard drive while making them easily accessible to yourself and to others. You can access the site from *www.flickr.com*. To get started, fill out the registration page and, if you wish, configure your profile. If you have friends who use Flickr, you can add them just as you do with Facebook. With that done, you can upload your first photos: click Organize & Create to get started.

SkyDrive is part of your Windows Live ID Internet presence and offers you an unbelievable 25 GB of storage space, for free! If your netbook has a small solid-state drive, it may not even offer that much storage space. To access SkyDrive you must first log into your Live account online. Visit *www. windowslive.com* to get started. Hover your mouse over the Windows Live option and click SkyDrive to access your personal storage area.

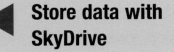
![Windows Live menu screenshot]

Windows Live™   Hotmail   Messenger   Office   Photos | MSN

- Home
- Devices
- SkyDrive
- Mobile
- Downloads
- All services

...with new Windows Ultimate laptop!

...| highlights

Send email   Calendar   Contacts   Options

You don't have any unread messages
Inbox | From contacts | Social updates | More ▾

Private messages (3)

If you've never heard of SkyDrive or aren't sure what it offers, here it is in a nutshell:

- SkyDrive is free with your Windows Live ID.

- SkyDrive offers 25 GB of online storage.

- You can password-protect your files so that only you can access them, or you can choose who to share files with if you desire. You can configure sharing on a per-file basis: it's not an all-or-nothing share configuration.

- SkyDrive works with Microsoft Office and lets you create, edit and share Microsoft Word, Excel, PowerPoint and OneNote files, online.

- You can easily upload photos and videos and share those files with others. You can even share with an entire social network. In fact, you can share files with individuals, groups, networks or no one at all.

- You can access SkyDrive from just about anywhere you can get online, including from most smart phones.

Store data with SkyDrive (cont.)

Storing data with SkyDrive

1 Log into your Windows Live page. There are various ways to get there, including *www.hotmail.com* and *www.live.com*.

2 Hover your mouse over the Windows Live icon and click SkyDrive.

3 Click New and click Folder.

4 Type a name for the folder, noting that by default it's not shared with anyone. Click Change if you want to share what you'll put in this folder with others. Click Next.

5 Position the SkyDrive window so that it takes up only half of the screen and position the window that contains the files to upload to take up the other half.

6 Drag and drop files as desired.

7 Click Continue. Note the new files.

■ You can upload data from your netbook or laptop, or from a web-enabled mobile phone. You can access data from the same devices.

■ You can view Microsoft Office files in a Web browser, without having to save the files to your computer's hard drive.

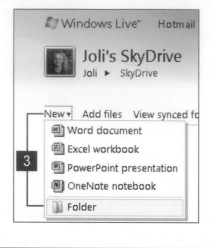

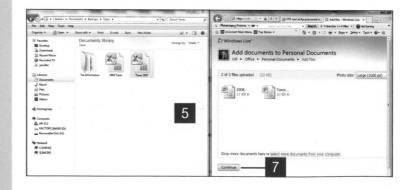

Personal Documents
Joli ▸ Office ▸ Personal Documents

New ▾   Add files   Share ▾   View: Details ▾   Sort by: Date ▾   Download as .zip file   More ▾

You've created the folder Personal Documents. Let people know

Today

📄 Taxes 2007   Joli Ballew   1 minute ago

📄 2008 Taxes   Edit in browser   Open in Excel   Share ▾   More ☐   ✕

8

Version history
Move
Copy
Rename
Download
Properties

Shared with: Just me

Here are a few more things you can expect:

- You can invite people to your workspace and let them access files you've marked for sharing, and they can work on those files if you wish.

- You can collaborate with others on Word documents, PowerPoint presentations and Excel spreadsheets from a web-based interface, thus maintaining version control.

- You can store files to the workspace that you would normally email to yourself or put on a flash drive for transfer.

- You can easily store and edit sensitive data online, enhancing security by keeping this data off your laptop or netbook.

- You can incorporate Windows Live Mesh, which enables you to sync data you've stored in SkyDrive with data on your computer. You can sync up to 5 GB of data.

If any of this interests you, perhaps using Live Mesh to sync files, or using SkyDrive to create Microsoft Office documents online, explore those options as time allows. For the most part, the interface is easy to use, but because features change so often it would be difficult to set out specific instructions here.

8 Explore as desired, noting you can click Share or More, among other things, to edit what you've uploaded.

For your information

ⓘ

You can't drag and drop entire folders, only files.

For your information

ⓘ

If you must have an on-board, installed office program, consider OpenOffice.org. It's a free, open-source office suite of programs you can use to create documents, spreadsheets, presentations and other file types. OpenOffice.org files are compatible with other office programs, including Microsoft Office.

Explore additional online resources

You can learn more about online storage, backup resources and 'in the cloud' technology online. Just search for 'online backups' or 'online office resources' to get started. You'll find there are lots of companies you can pay for backup services, as well as many free resources that can help you get more from your laptop or netbook. You can also search for 'netbook resources' to learn how to get more from your laptop or netbook.

Here are a few things to explore further, most of which are free (but things do change frequently):

- Dropbox – another option for online storage. It's a basic drop box, enabling you to upload and download data as needed, and to back up sensitive data as desired. As with similar offerings from other companies, you can also sync and share data, among other things.

- Google Docs – here you can upload files, access uploaded data from anywhere, share your work and collaborate with others in real time, insert photos from Picasa (detailed later in this list), drag and drop files, and more.

- Mozy Online Backup – this is a paid backup service that you can use to back up everything on your laptop or netbook. You can configure automatic backups, encrypt backups, even easily restore your computer from backups.

- GoToMyPC – this program enables you to access your home computer from your laptop or netbook provided you have a connection to the Internet. It's easy to set up, and once you are connected, you can access the data on your home computer just as easily as if you were sitting in front of it. At the time of writing there's a free 30-day trial.

- Picasa 3 – you can upload photos and edit them, organise them in albums and share those photos with others. You'll have access to 1 GB of storage, enough to store more than 400,000 pictures.

Exploring additional online resources

17

1 Using any web browser, perform a search for 'must have netbook apps'.

2 Read through the results, looking for a list that contains any of the options listed here.

3 Click any link to learn more about any program or resource.

Appendix: choose a laptop or netbook

Introduction

If you've yet to purchase a laptop or netbook or are considering replacing what you have, read through the tips in this Appendix. There are lots of things to consider, including its weight and size, cost and related features, Internet connection options, and things such as the amount of RAM, hard drive space and processor speed. You'll also want to consider laptop bags, additional batteries, extended warranties and set-up services.

What you'll do

Visit a computer store and ask questions

Check out the manufacturer's website

Make the purchase

If you're shopping for a laptop or netbook or if you're considering replacing an older desktop PC, there are several things to weigh up before you buy. If you're planning to travel via plane, for instance, you'll want to research the computer's weight and size. The smaller and lighter the laptop or netbook is, the easier it will be to travel with. If you travel mostly in an RV or car, weight and size may not be an issue. In both cases, though, the laptop or netbook needs to be large enough so that you can use it easily, making these factors even more complex. You'll also want to consider cost, features, speed and how the keyboard feels when you type on it.

Weight and size

A typical laptop weighs 4–8lb. Netbooks often weigh 3–4lb. As you know, though, netbooks lack features laptops have, such as DVD drives. When purchasing a portable computer, then, make sure it's not too heavy but contains the features you really need. For instance, if you really do need a DVD player, make sure you get one, even if you have to purchase a heavier and more expensive laptop.

You should also consider its physical size. When a portable computer is too small, it may be hard to use the keyboard and pointing device, especially if you're a big person. You might consider carrying a small mouse with you on your travels if you find this is the case, or if you decide you really do want a netbook but can't manage the small track pad.

Ergonomics

You'll want to test the keyboard before you buy a laptop or netbook. The finest netbook will become a burden if you can't type effectively. This happens more often than you think; I have a laptop whose keyboard is so hard to use that I actually bring along an external keyboard and mouse, and connect them using the laptop's USB ports. This defeats the main purpose of the laptop, of course: portability and convenience.

A laptop or netbook's small size can make it uncomfortable to use. Often, your laptop's display is not set at eye level, and the keyboard is not properly positioned for best posture. If possible, try to improve your position by putting the laptop or netbook on a desk, raising or lowering your chair while at a desk, or building a special table or tray for use while sitting in an easy chair or on a couch.

Cost and features

PC desktop towers are often less expensive than laptops and are more easily upgradable if you need or want additional features later. Because it's nearly impossible to add features internally to a small netbook or larger laptop, for instance a DVD drive, FireWire port or larger hard drive, it's important to find a computer you really like and which offers the features you want right from the beginning. I'll spell out later what you should look for, but make sure you save enough money to get the power and features you need and not simply any

Visiting a computer store and asking questions

1 If you're close to a computer store, visit in person.

2 At the store, ask the following questions:
   a. What is your least expensive laptop or netbook?
   b. What is your most expensive laptop or netbook?
   c. What are the differences?
   d. What features are absolutely necessary?
   e. What features are not necessary?

3 Tell the salesperson how you plan to use the laptop or netbook.

old computer you can afford. One thing you'll need to decide is whether you like the touchpad offered in many laptops, or perhaps you'd like to shop for something else. Many people have a touchpad but connect a mouse. It's up to you.

4 Ask the salesperson the following questions:

a. What laptop or netbook would you suggest?

b. Will a less expensive model work?

c. Is this laptop or netbook rugged enough for what I want to do?

d. Can you show me any independent reviews of this laptop or netbook?

5 Leave the store without buying anything, spend a day or two mulling it over and reviewing your options, then return to make the purchase if you wish.

Reliability

Laptops and netbooks are more prone to accidents than desktops because you take them with you, and they can be damaged if they are exposed to too much heat, humidity or vibration. Of course, a laptop can be stolen, lost or left behind, too. When considering a portable computer, then, know that you'll have to be extremely careful with it and keep it safe from harm. Get one you feel you can easily carry, pack and manage. Make sure, when you purchase a laptop or netbook, that you can secure it with a lock, preferably a Kensington lock, and buy that lock if you plan to travel.

Connectivity

When purchasing a laptop or netbook, make sure it includes Ethernet and wireless networking. You don't know where your travels will take you, so it's best to be prepared for any type of connection. Here's an Ethernet cable icon. On a side note, if you think you'll need a modem, make sure the computer you choose offers this, too.

I can't tell you exactly what you'll need in a laptop or netbook, but I can help you choose one by providing a list of things you'll probably want. Here are some things to consider:

- A capable processor – almost all laptops and netbooks have a processor that is fast enough to handle email, web surfing, uploading and viewing photos, and keeping a journal. That said, you may not need to purchase a computer with the fastest processor to get one you'll love. If you plan to render movies in Movie Maker, though, or if you need to use Photoshop or other high-end graphics programs, you'll need a faster processor than what you'll find in your basic netbook or low-end laptop.

- Additional processors – if you play games that require lots of calculations, create your own movies, or perform other resource-intensive tasks (you'll know if you do), consider a computer with dual processors. Some laptops come with dual processors or graphics cards with processors built in.

- More RAM – random access memory is where your laptop or netbook will temporarily store information while it processes it. You should get a netbook that has at least 1 gigabyte (GB) of memory. Get more if you can afford it. Laptops should come with 2 GB or more. Again, more is always better in this case.

- Hard drive space – a hard drive is where your data is stored. Digital music, photos and video take up a surprisingly large amount of hard drive space. Make sure you get at least 160 GB of hard drive space, and get more if you can afford it. If you're opting for a solid-state drive, get the largest capacity drive you can afford.

- Size and weight – carefully consider a laptop or netbook's weight. Although 7lb may not feel like a heavy piece of equipment now, after carrying it along with a power cable, adapters, computer case and other peripherals from your car to the airport terminal, you'll be wishing you'd opted for the 4lb model. Trust me on this.

- Battery life – always look at battery life and if you can't afford a model that offers long battery life, get an extra battery or an extended battery.

◀ **Shopping checklist**

For your information

The best way to compare battery life, weight, processor speed, RAM and other components is to go to an electronics store where laptops and netbooks are offered side by side, and where you can compare price and features.

Shopping checklist (cont.)

■ Wireless – the laptop should have Ethernet and wireless capabilities. Be careful, though, the salesperson may try to sell you a wireless Internet plan, often in the form of a two-year contract. This may or may not be a competitive price, and the coverage area may not suit your needs. Don't buy any wireless service until you've had time to fully explore your options and research coverage and pricing.

■ Dimensions – the size of the screen is a big part of selecting a laptop or netbook. It may seem that a 17-inch or 19-inch screen is the way to go, until you try to use it on a plane. And a 12.5-inch or 15-inch screen may seem perfect for you, too, until you want to do some image editing. Of course, it's likely the larger screen size will cause the weight of the laptop or netbook to increase. You'll have to carefully weigh where and how you'll use your laptop or netbook before deciding on a screen size.

■ DVD drive – if you want a DVD player for watching movies, you'll have to get a larger laptop. If possible, spend the extra money to get a DVD-writeable drive if you're going down that route. If you're looking at netbooks, consider online movie options such as Lovefilm if you want to watch movies using your new portable computer.

To sum up, here's what you'll want to look for if:

- you simply want to check email, surf the web, keep a journal and upload a picture or two: compare prices of brand-name computers. Any laptop or netbook these days can handle these tasks, no matter how slow the processor or how little RAM (provided it's new, that is). Make sure, if you buy a lower-end laptop or netbook, that it comes with Ethernet and wireless capabilities.

- you travel a lot: focus on weight, battery life and how well the keyboard responds to your typing style. Make sure you get at least 1 GB of RAM, a 160 GB hard drive and wireless capabilities. Get more of anything you can afford, though, especially RAM.

- you play a lot of games: make sure you get a computer with a high-end graphics chip, graphics card and powerful processor. You'll also want a 17-inch or larger high-resolution monitor.

- you love all things media and/or want to create home movies: focus on getting a large hard drive (500 GB), dual core processor and 3 GB+ of RAM. You may even want to purchase an external hard drive, shown here.

Shopping checklist (cont.)

Checking out the manufacturer's website

1. After you've selected the laptop or netbook you want to buy, or have narrowed it down to a few makes and models, visit the manufacturer's website(s).

2. Browse through the site. Look for Support and/or Help pages.

3. See whether there is an online or chat option for getting support.

4. Call the manufacturer's help line to see how long it takes to talk to a support person.

5. See how expensive additional components are, such as extra RAM, external speakers and the like.

6. See how much it would cost to purchase the laptop through this website versus the store. Remember to take into account any shipping charges.

Choosing a rugged laptop

Making the purchase

1 Make sure the laptop or netbook you've selected fully meets your needs.

2 Do not purchase an additional warranty or sign up for any 'services'. You can load anti-virus software, configure a screen saver and input your user name yourself.

3 Purchase an additional battery if you think you will be travelling away from power sources often.

4 Purchase an Ethernet cable and keep it with you.

5 If you will be away from power sources for extended periods, consider purchasing a second battery.

6 Consider purchasing a laptop desk.

7 Look over Internet subscription plans if you don't have one. Don't purchase a plan at the store, though, just look at your options.

8 Look at computer bags. You're going to want one that can hold all of your peripherals, is padded and has a shoulder strap.

9 If you don't already have one, purchase a surge protector.

Yes, there is such a thing as a rugged laptop. You'll want to consider a rugged laptop if you plan to take your laptop with you on a safari or mountain-climbing excursion, for instance. Rugged laptops have sealed keyboards and casings and are thus better protected from water, humidity, sand and dust. Even the external ports are protected with plastic covers.

Rugged laptops also have a stronger outer shell, offering internal protection for the CPU, hard disk drive and optical drives. This means, if you drop it, it's less likely to be damaged, and it's less susceptible to shock and vibration than regular laptops are. Many rugged laptops can also repel rain, snow, sleet, hail, wind, fog, dust, sand, extreme cold and heat, salt spray and/or humidity.

There's no doubt you'll be asked to buy an extended warranty when you buy your laptop or netbook. This warranty is supposed to cover everything from drops to spills to hard drive crashes to mechanical failures. Don't fall for this scam. It's highly unlikely you'll need the coverage, and highly unlikely you'll be covered if something does happen.

An extended warranty is supposed to act as an insurance package. The multi-page document you'll sign when you purchase it will explain what the extended warranty covers. If you really are sold on the idea of an extended warranty, ask to see the agreement. Read it carefully, ask questions and beware of vague references to what 'damage' is covered. If you really want to insure your laptop or netbook, consider your home or car insurance company, or opt for a company that is in the business of covering electronics.

Extended warranties

Jargon buster

Activation – The process you must complete to verify you have a valid copy of Windows 7, including a proper product ID. You usually activate Windows 7 online, the first time you turn on the computer. This is mandatory.

Adware – Internet advertisements (which are also applications) that often include additional code that can be used to track a user's personal information and pass it on to third parties, without the user's authorisation or knowledge.

Aero – Builds on the basic Windows 7 interface and offers a high-performing desktop experience that includes (among other things) the translucent effect of Aero Glass.

Aero Glass – Added visual reflections and soft animations that are applied when an Aero theme is selected as the display setting.

Applications – Software installed on your computer other than the operating system. Some applications come preinstalled, such as Internet Explorer. Third-party applications are software you purchase separately and install yourself, for instance Microsoft Office or Photoshop.

AV-in – Accepts input from various audio/video devices.

Backup and Restore Center – Lets you perform backups, and in the case of a laptop failure, restore them (put them back). However, there are other backup options, too, including copying files to a CD or DVD, copying pictures and media to an external hard drive, USB drive or memory card, or storing them on an Internet server.

Bandwidth – Generally this is used to represent how much data you send and receive on a paid connection, such as a smart phone or Internet connection.

Battery bay – This holds the laptop's battery. Sometimes you have to use a screwdriver to get inside the battery bay, other times you simply need to slide out the compartment door.

Battery lock – This locks the battery in position.

Battery release latch – This holds the battery in place, even after the battery bay's door has been opened. You'll need to release this latch to get to the battery.

Bluetooth – A technology used to create 'personal' networks for the purpose of connecting devices that are in close range (such as a mobile phone and an earpiece). A laptop may come with built-in Bluetooth capabilities (although this is not common), or you can add it by purchasing and installing a USB Bluetooth dongle.

Bluetooth dongle – A small device, about the size of a USB flash drive, which connects directly to a USB port on the outside of the laptop.

Boot up – When a laptop or netbook is powered on, it goes through a sequence of tasks before you see the Desktop. This process is called the boot-up process. Laptops can be rated by many factors, and one of those factors is how long the boot-up process takes.

Browse – Browsing for a file, folder or program is the process of drilling down into the Windows 7 folder structure to locate the desired item.

Burn – A term used to describe the process of copying music from a laptop to a CD or DVD. Generally, music is burned to a CD, since CDs can be played in cars and generic CD players, and videos are burned to DVDs, since they require much more space and can be played on DVD players.

Contacts folder – Contains your contacts' information, which includes email addresses, pictures, phone numbers, home and businesses addresses, and more.

Control Panel – Available in all Windows 7 editions, a place where you can change laptop settings related to system and maintenance, user accounts, security, appearance, networks and the Internet, the time, language and region, hardware and sounds, visual displays and accessibility options, programs and additional options.

Cookies – Small text files that include data that identifies your preferences when you visit particular websites. Cookies are what allow you to visit, say, *www.amazon.com* and be greeted with Hello <your name>, We have recommendations for you! Cookies help a site offer you a personalised web experience.

Copy command – Copies the data to Windows 7's clipboard (a virtual, temporary holding area). The data will be not deleted from its original location even when you 'paste' it somewhere else. Pasting Copy data will copy the data, not move it.

CPU – Central processing unit. This is the 'computer chip' inside your laptop.

Cut – To remove the selected text, picture or object.

Cut command – Copies the data to Windows 7's clipboard (a virtual, temporary holding area). The data will be deleted from its original location as soon as you 'paste' it somewhere else. Pasting Cut data moves the data.

Desktop folder – Contains links to items for data you have created on your Desktop, as well as familiar Desktop items such as the Recycle Bin.

Dialogue box – A place to make changes to default settings in an application. Clicking File and then Print, for instance, opens the Print dialogue box where you can configure the type of paper you're using, select a printer, and more.

Disk Cleanup – An application included with Windows 7 that offers a safe and effective way to reduce unnecessary data on your computer. With Disk Cleanup you can remove temporary files, empty the Recycle Bin, remove set-up log files and downloaded program files (among other things), all in a single process.

Disk Defragmenter – An application included with Windows 7 that analyses the data stored on your hard drive and consolidates files that are not stored together. This enhances performance by making data on your hard drive work faster by making data easier to access. Disk Defragmenter runs automatically once a week, in the middle of the night.

Downloads folder – Does not contain anything by default but offers a place to save items you download from the Internet, such as drivers and third-party programs.

DPI – Dots per inch refers to the number of dots (or pixels) per inch on a computer monitor.

Driver – A piece of software (or code) that allows the device to communicate with Windows 7 and vice versa.

DV – Digital video, generally used as DV camera.

DVD drive – A physical piece of equipment that can play and often record DVDs.

DVI port – Used to connect the laptop to a television set or other DVI device. For laptops, this is generally an upscale display.

Email address – A virtual address you use for sending and receiving email. It often takes this form: *yourname@ yourispname.com*.

Enhancements – Features in Windows Media Player that you can use to enhance your music, including a graphic equaliser.

Ergonomics – The science of working without causing injury to yourself. Injury can include back strain, eye strain, or carpal tunnel syndrome, among others.

Ethernet – A technology that uses Ethernet cables to transmit data and network laptops.

Ethernet cable – Used to connect computers to routers and cable modems, among other things.

Extended warranty – A warranty that you purchase along with the manufacturer's warranty. This type of warranty is supposed to cover everything, including drops and spills. Often, though, extended warranties fail to pay in such an event (which is spelled out in the fine print).

FireWire – Also called IEEE 1394, a technology often used to connect digital video cameras, professional audio hardware and external hard drives to a computer. FireWire connections are much faster than USB, and are better than anything else when you need to transfer large amounts of data, such as digital video.

Flip and Flip 3-D – A way to move through open windows graphically instead of clicking the item in the Taskbar.

Form data – In Internet Explorer, this is information that's been saved using Internet Explorer's autocomplete form data functionality. If you don't want forms to be filled out automatically by you or someone else who has access to your computer and user account, delete this.

Gadget – In our terms, an icon such as the Weather or Clock gadget, available from the Desktop Gadget Gallery.

GHz – Short for gigahertz, this term describes how fast a processor can work. 1 GHz equals 1 billion cycles per second, so a 2.4 GHz computer chip will execute calculations at 240 billion cycles per second. Again, it's only important to know that the faster the chip, the faster the computer.

GPU – Short for graphics processing unit, it's a processor used specifically for rendering graphics. Having a processor just for graphics frees up the main CPU, allowing it to work faster on other tasks.

Hard drive – A physical piece of equipment where your data is stored. Hard drives are inside a laptop, but you can purchase additional, external hard drives to back up data. Digital music, photos and video take up a surprisingly large amount of hard drive space.

History – In Internet Explorer, this is the list of websites you've visited and any web addresses you've typed. Anyone who has access to your computer and user account can look at your History list to see where you've been.

Hotspot – A Wi-Fi hotspot lets you connect to the Internet without having to be tethered to an Ethernet cable or tied down with a high monthly wireless bill. Sometimes this service is free, provided you have the required wireless hardware.

Icon – A visual representation of a file or folder that you can click to open it.

Instant messaging – Text and instant messaging require you to type your message and click a Send button. It's similar to email, but it's instantaneous and more conversation-like – the recipient gets the message right after you send it and responds. Instant messaging is the term generally reserved for text communications between two or more computers; text messaging is a term generally reserved for communicating between two mobile phones.

Interface – What you see on the screen when working in a window. In Paint's interface, you see the Menu bar, Toolbox and Color box.

Internet – A large web of computers that communicates via routers for the purpose of sharing information and data. Also called the World Wide Web.

Internet server – A computer that stores data off site. Windows Live offers Internet servers to hold email and data so that you do not have to store when on your computer. Internet servers allow you to access information from any computer that can access the Internet.

ISP – Internet service provider. A company that provides Internet access, usually for a fee.

Kensington lock slot – A way to connect the laptop to a lock to prevent it from being stolen from a hotel or RV.

Line-in jack – An input on a laptop that accepts audio from external devices, such as CD players.

Link – A shortcut to a web page. Links are often offered in an email, document or web page to allow you to access a site without having to actually type in its name. In almost all instances, links are underlined and in a different colour than the page they are configured on.

Load – A web page must 'load' before you can access it. Some pages load instantly while others take a few seconds.

Mail server – A computer that your email provider configures to allow you to send and receive email. It often includes a POP3 incoming mail server and an SMTP outgoing mail server. Often the server names look something like *pop.yourispnamehere.com* and *smtp. yourispnamehere.com.*

Malware – Stands for malicious software. Malware includes viruses, worms, spyware, etc.

Menu – A title on a menu bar (such as File, Edit, View). Clicking this menu button opens a drop-down list with additional choices (Open, Save, Print).

Menu bar – A bar that runs across the top of an application that offers menus. Often, these menus include File, Edit, View, Insert, Format and Help.

Modem port – A port on the outside of a laptop that lets you connect your laptop to a phone jack using a standard telephone cord. Allows you to connect to the Internet using a dial-up connection.

Network – A group of computers, printers and other devices that communicates wirelessly or through wired connections.

Network (from the Start menu) – The Network window offers links to computers on your network and the Network and Sharing Center. You can also add printers and wireless devices here.

Network adapter – A piece of hardware that lets your computer connect to a network, such as the Internet or a local network.

Network and Sharing Center – A collection of features where you can easily access network connections, sharing options, networked computers and devices, and diagnose and repair features.

Network Discovery – a state where computers can find other computers on the network. Network Discovery must be on to locate and communicate with network devices.

Network map – Details each of your network connections graphically and allows you to distinguish easily among wired, wireless and Internet connections. It's available from the Network and Sharing Center.

Notification area – The area of the Taskbar that includes the clock and the volume icons, and also holds icons for applications that are running in the background. You may see icons for your anti-virus software, music players, updates, or Windows security alerts.

Operating system – In this case, the operating system is Windows 7. This is what allows you to operate your computer's system. You will use Windows 7 to find things you have stored on your laptop, connect to the Internet, send and receive email, and surf the Web, among other things.

Paste command – Copies or moves the cut or copied data to the new location. If the data was cut, it will be moved. If the data was copied, it will be copied.

Per user archived Windows Error Reporting – Files used for error reporting and solution checking.

Phishing – A technique used by computer hackers to get you to divulge personal information such as bank account numbers. Phishing filters warn you of potential phishing websites and email, and are included in Windows 7. To put it another way, phishing is an attempt by a unscrupulous website or hacker to obtain personal data including but not limited to bank account numbers, social security numbers and email addresses.

Pixel – The smallest unit in which data can be displayed on a computer. Resolution is defined by how many pixels you choose to display.

Playlist – A group of songs that you can save and then listen to as a group, burn to a CD, copy to a portable music player, and more.

POP3 server name – The name of the computer that you will use to get your email from your email provider. Your ISP or email provider will give you this information when you subscribe.

Power cable – The cable that you will use to connect the laptop to the wall outlet (power outlet). You can connect and disconnect the power cable at any time, even when the laptop is running.

Power plan – A group of settings that you can configure to tell Windows 7 when and if to turn off the computer monitor or display, and when or if to put the laptop to sleep.

Print button – Clicking Print opens the Print dialogue box where you can configure the page range, select a printer, change page orientation, change print order, and choose a paper type. Additional options include print quality, output bins, and more. Of course, the choices offered depend on what your printer offers. If your printer can print at only 300 × 300 dots per inch, you can't configure it to print at a higher quality.

Print Preview button – Clicking Print Preview opens a window where you can see before you print what the printout will actually look like. You can switch between portrait and landscape views, access the Page Setup dialogue box, and more.

Processor – Short for microprocessor, it's the silicon chip that contains the central processing unit (CPU) inside a computer. Generally, the terms CPU and processor are used interchangeably. The CPU does almost all of the computer's calculations and is the most important piece of hardware in a computer system.

Programs – See Applications.

Public folders – Folders where you can share data. Anyone with an account on the laptop can access the data inside these folders. You can also configure Public folders to share files with people using other computers on your local network.

RAM – Short for random access memory, it's the hardware inside your laptop that temporarily stores data that is being used by the operating system or programs. Although there are many types of RAM, all you need to know is that the more RAM you have, the faster your laptop will (theoretically) run and perform.

Ready Boost – A new technology that lets you improve your computer's performance. The result is similar to adding RAM, but technically, Ready Boost is not RAM.

Recycle Bin – Holds deleted files until you decide to empty it. The Recycle Bin serves as a safeguard, allowing you to recover items accidentally deleted, or items you thought you no longer wanted but later decide you need. Note that once you empty the Recycle Bin, the items in it are gone for ever.

Registration – A non-mandatory task that you generally perform during the Windows 7 activation process. By registering you can get email about Windows 7 and new products. Registration is not mandatory.

Resolution – How many pixels are shown on a computer screen. Choosing 800 × 600 pixels means that the Desktop is shown to you with 800 pixels across and 600 pixels down. When you increase the resolution, you increase the number of pixels on the screen.

Rip – A term used to describe the process of copying files from a physical CD to your hard drive and thus your music library.

Router – A piece of equipment used to send data from laptop to computer on a network. A router 'routes' the data to the correct computer and also rejects data that is harmful or from unknown sources.

Screen saver – A picture or animation that covers your screen and appears after your laptop has been idle for a specific length of time that you set. You can configure your screen saver to require a password on waking up for extra security.

SD card slots or card readers – Slots on the outside of the laptop used to accept digital memory cards found in digital cameras and similar technologies.

Setup Log Files – Files created by Windows during set-up processes.

SMTP server name – The name of the computer that you will use to send email using your email service provider's servers. Your email provider will give you this information when you subscribe.

Spam – Unwanted email. Compare spam to junk faxes or junk postal mail.

Surge protector – A piece of hardware you use to protect the computer from power surges.

Surges – Unexpected increases in the voltage of an electrical current. Surges have the potential to damage sensitive electrical equipment. (Sags are the opposite of surges, equally dangerous, and are a drop in electrical current.)

S-Video – A port or technology used to connect the laptop to a television or other display that also offers s-video connectivity.

Sync – The process of comparing data in one location to the data in another and performing tasks to match it up. If data has been added or deleted from one device, for instance, synching can also add or delete it from the other.

System archived Windows Error Reporting – Files used for error reporting and solution checking.

System Restore – If enabled, Windows 7 stores 'restore points' on your computer's hard drive. If something goes wrong you can run System Restore, choose one of these points and revert to a pre-problem date. Since System Restore deals only with 'system data', none of your personal data will be affected (not even your last email).

System Restore Point – A snapshot of the laptop that Windows 7 keeps in case something happens and you need to revert to it because of a bad installation or hardware driver.

Tags – Data about a particular piece of data, such as a photo or a song or album. Tags can be used to group pictures or music in various ways. Some tags are applied automatically when you import pictures from a digital camera, including the date they were uploaded, along with any name you applied to the imported group. You can create your own tags.

Taskbar – The bar that runs horizontally across the bottom of the Windows 7 interface and contains the Start button and Notification area. It also offers a place to view and access open files, folders and applications.

Temporary Files – Files created and stored by programs for use by the program. Most of these temporary files are deleted when you exit the program, but some remain.

Temporary Internet files – Files that contain copies of web pages you've visited on your hard drive, so that you can view the pages more quickly when visiting the page again.

Thumbnails – Small icons of your pictures, videos and documents. Thumbnails will be recreated as needed should you choose to delete them using Disk Cleanup.

Touchpad – A pointing device that is usually located in the centre of the keyboard or at the bottom of it. Place your finger on the touchpad or trackball and move it around to move the mouse.

USB – Universal serial bus, a port you use to connect USB devices. USB devices include mice, external keyboards, mobile phones, digital cameras, and other devices, including USB flash drives.

VGA port – An external monitor port. With this port you can connect your laptop to a secondary monitor or network projector where you can mirror what you see on the laptop's screen or extend the screen to the second monitor. A VGA port is a 15-pin port.

Video format – The video file type, such as AVI or WMA.

Video messaging – A form of instant messaging where one or both users also offer live video of themselves during the conversation.

Virus – A self-replicating program that infects laptops with intent to do harm. Viruses often come in the form of an attachment in an email.

Visualisations – Produced by Windows 7 and Windows Media Player, these are graphical representations of the music you play.

Web browser – Windows 7 comes with Internet Explorer, an application you can use to surf the Internet. Internet Explorer has everything you need, including a pop-up blocker, zoom settings and accessibility options, as well as tools you can use to save your favourite web pages, set home pages and sign up for RSS feeds.

Webcam – A camera that can send live images over the Internet.

Website – A group of web pages that contains related information. Microsoft's website has information about Microsoft products, for instance.

Window – When you open a program from the Start menu, a document, folder or picture, it opens in a 'window'. Window, as it's used in this context, is synonymous with an open program, file or folder and has nothing to do with the word Windows, used with Windows 7.

Windows Defender – You don't have to do much to Windows Defender except understand that it offers protection against Internet threats. It's enabled by default and it runs in the background. However, if you ever think your laptop has been attacked by an Internet threat (virus, worm, malware, etc.) you can run a manual scan here.

Windows Firewall – If enabled and configured properly, the firewall will help prevent hackers (people whose job it is to get into your laptop and do harm to it) from accessing your computer and data.

The firewall blocks most programs from communicating outside the network (or outside your computer). If you want to allow a program to communicate outside your safety zone you can 'allow' a program by adding it to an 'exceptions' list. This is all very easy to do.

Windows Media Center – Available in Windows 7 Home Premium or higher, an application that allows you to watch, pause and record live television, locate, download and/or listen to music and radio, view, edit and share photos and videos, and play DVDs (among other things).

Windows Mobility Center – An application that lets you adjust your mobile computer or laptop settings quickly, including things like volume, wireless features and brightness.

Windows Update – If enabled and configured properly, when you are online Windows 7 will check for security updates automatically and install them. You don't have to do anything, and your computer is always updated with the latest security patches and features.

Worm – A self-replicating program that infects laptops with intent to do harm. However, unlike a virus, it does not need to attach itself to a running program.

Troubleshooting guide